RETHINKING THE WORLD
—DARE TO KNOW—

激動の現代社会を読み解く視点

FRANÇOIS DE SOETE

SEIBIDO

音声ファイルのダウンロード／ストリーミング

CD マーク表示がある箇所は、音声を弊社 HP より無料でダウンロード／ストリーミングすることができます。下記 URL の書籍詳細ページに音声ダウンロードアイコンがございますのでそちらから自習用音声としてご活用ください。

https://seibido.co.jp/ad670

Rethinking the World
— Dare to Know —

Preface

Every generation witnesses a few key moments that precipitate radical changes to a particular country, region, and, at times, even the whole world. In some cases, a largely positive development leads to profound changes in the way that people think about the world. Neil Armstrong helped redefine what is possible when he famously became the first person to set foot on the Moon in 1969, for example, while Mahatma Gandhi's nonviolent resistance movement that led to the end of British rule in India in 1947 helped inspire decolonization efforts throughout the world. In other cases, terrible events forever change the way that people see the world. The Second World War revealed just how much devastation modern weapons and warfare could unleash, while the 9/11 terrorist attacks in the United States exposed just how vulnerable free societies are to violent extremists.

Several recent events have had a profound impact on Japan and on the world. Most notably, the novel coronavirus first detected in Wuhan, China, in late 2019 that then spread to become a global pandemic in early 2020 transformed societies throughout the world. Though several high-profile events have had a dramatic impact on the world since then, and surely other impactful events will occur in the coming decades, this global pandemic will likely go down in history as one of the most transformative events of the twenty-first century. There is no denying that the COVID-19 pandemic has altered the way that we think about the world, but the reality is that countless changes, big and small, are constantly occurring that reshape the world in one way or another. With this theme of change serving as a backdrop, each of the twenty chapters that comprise this book focuses on a particular topic and considers it in the context of relevant changes that may be on the horizon.

One thing that has remained constant in our ever-changing world, with "the world" being used here in a literal and a figurative sense, is the prevalence of English as a global language. The need for a common language is obvious as the world grows increasingly interconnected, and so this book is designed to help readers grow more comfortable applying their English language skills to a wide variety of themes—ranging from relatively light and casual topics to subjects that are notably more profound and serious in nature. Each chapter presents information about a particular topic, along with exercises that are designed to help readers not only develop their English language skills, but their critical thinking skills as well. Each chapter, in effect, can thereby help readers formulate reasoned and informed opinions in English about the topic being covered.

Two thousand years ago, in his *Epistles*, the Roman poet Horace wrote: *sapere aude*—which is a Latin phrase commonly translated as "dare to know." The German philosopher Immanuel Kant later made this Latin phrase emblematic of the Enlightenment when in 1784 he published an essay espousing the virtues that were spreading in Europe at the time: political liberty, the use of reason, and the quest for knowledge. "Dare to know" is a fitting statement here as well, for it will hopefully encourage you to become more informed about the issues covered in this book, and the knowledge that you acquire here should prove helpful as you begin rethinking the world.

François de Soete

はしがき

　どの時代にも、特定の国や地域、時には世界全体に劇的な変化をもたらす重要な瞬間がいくつかあるものだ。時には、概して前向きな進展が、人々の世界に対する考え方に大きな変化をもたらすことがある。例えば、ニール・アームストロングは1969年に世界で初めて月面に降り立ち、何が可能かを再定義し、マハトマ・ガンジーは非暴力抵抗運動によって1947年にインドにおける英国の支配を終わらせ、世界中の脱植民地化の取り組みに刺激を与えた。また、悲惨な出来事が、人々の世界の見方を一変させることもある。第二次世界大戦は、近代の兵器や戦争がどれほどの惨状をもたらすかを明らかにし、米国で起きた9.11の同時多発テロは、自由な社会が暴力的な過激派に対していかに脆弱であるかを露呈した。

　最近のいくつかの出来事は、日本や世界に大きな影響を与えた。最も注目すべきは、2019年後半に中国の武漢で初めて検出された新型コロナウィルスが、2020年初頭に世界的なパンデミックとなり、世界中を一変させたことだ。その後、いくつかの注目すべき出来事が世界に大きな影響を与え、今後数十年の間に他にも衝撃的な出来事が起こることは間違いないだろうが、この世界的なパンデミックは、21世紀で最も変革をもたらした出来事の一つとして歴史に刻まれる可能性が高い。新型コロナウィルスの大流行が私たちの世界観を変えたことは否定できないが、現実には大小を問わず数えきれない変化が常に起きていて、それが世界を作り替えている。本書では、この「変化」というテーマを背景に、20の各章で特定のトピックに焦点を当て、目前に迫った変化との関連で考察している。

　絶え間なく変化するこの世界（ここでは「世界」を文字通りの意味でも、比喩的な意味でも使っている）で変わらないことの一つは、グローバル言語としての英語の普及である。世界がますます相互に結びついていく中で、共通言語の必要性は明らかである。そのため本書は、比較的易しい形式ばらない話題から核心を突くような重大な話題まで、英語のスキルをさまざまなテーマに活かすことができるよう構成されている。各章には、特定のトピックに関する情報とともに、英語力だけでなく批判的思考力を養うためのエクササイズが付されている。各章とも、読者がそのトピックについて英語で論理的かつ十分な情報に基づいた意見を述べることができるよう作られている。

　今から2000年前、ローマの詩人ホラティウスが『書簡詩』の中で“sapere aude（サペレ・アウデー）”という言葉を残した。これはラテン語で、英語では一般的に“dare to know（知識を得ることに勇気を持て）”と訳されている。ドイツの哲学者イマヌエル・カントは、後にこの言葉を啓蒙主義の象徴とし、当時ヨーロッパに広まっていた政治的自由、理性の行使、知識の探求といった美徳を唱えたエッセイを1784年に発表している。本書においても、読者のみなさんの知識欲を駆り立てるのを促すという意味でふさわしい表現だ。ここで得た知識を、世界を見つめ直す際に役立ててもらえれば幸いである。

　最後に、本書の企画・編集にあたりお世話になった成美堂編集部の工藤隆志氏と太田裕美氏に謝意を表したい。

François de Soete

本書の使い方

各章の構成は以下のとおりとなっている。

導入

　各章の冒頭に日本語で本文の主題や背景説明が簡潔に書かれている。あまりなじみのないテーマであったとしても、この日本語による簡単な説明や問いを読むことで興味を持つことができる。

Getting Started

　このセクションは、本文を読み始める前に、その準備として関連内容について学生が各自で考えることのできる質問を用意してある。個人の意見を問うものであるので、下調べ等の必要はない。授業内でディスカッションのテーマとして利用することも可能である。

Reading

　わかりやすい英文で書かれた本文は、文化や社会問題、環境、国際ニュースや政治、科学や人間・宇宙の起源から哲学まで、幅広いトピックを扱っている。予備知識がなくても十分に理解できる内容となっている。また、『大学英語教育学会　基本語リスト』（通称 JACET 8000）の基本的には5000 語レベル以上および固有名詞に注釈をつけている。

Vocabulary

　本文で使用された語について、それぞれの意味を選択する問題。知らない単語であっても、辞書を使うのではなく、文中で使用されている箇所を読みながら解答を推測するように指示している。また、単語の意味を英語で説明できるようになるための訓練としても使うことができる。

Comprehension Questions

　本文の内容理解を問う問題。本文の該当箇所を特定すれば答えられる易しめの問題だけではなく、本文の内容と問題文の意味をよく理解していなければ解答できない難しめのものも用意してあるので、内容分析の力も養うことができる。

Putting It All Together

　本文の各パラグラフの要約を書く問題。抜き書きするのではなく、自分の言葉で書くよう指示をしているため、内容理解と同時に作文力も養うことができる。

Debating the Issues

　本文に関連した質問に対して自分の意見を述べる問題。ライティングの宿題としても授業内でのディスカッションにも使用できる。なぜそのように考えたのか理由も述べて議論を深めることができるようになっている。

Point of Interest

　本文で扱っているテーマや人物に関連した、おもしろい豆知識を平易な英文でまとめたコラム。本文の関連箇所に、日本語でこの欄への参照指示が掲載されており、関心に応じて読み進めることができる。CD を聴きながら空欄になっている単語を埋めるリスニングとディクテーションの問題にもなっており、単語や語尾の変化の聞き取りとつづりの練習になっている。

Table of Contents

THE ART OF PERSUASION

What is the key to making a good argument?

千年以上も昔の哲学者が、今日の私たちに説得力のある議論の仕方について実践的な助言ができるとは信じがたいかもしれない。しかし、ある有名な哲学者は、現代でも有効な方法を示唆してくれる。相手を説得するにはどうすればよいと彼は述べているのか。また、他人が私たちを説得しようとするメカニズムを理解する際に、彼の助言はどのように役立つだろうか。

The ability to make a convincing argument is a key part of academic work, whether in the form of a presentation or in the form of a written research paper.

▌ GETTING STARTED

Think about the question below and then write a short response. There is no right or wrong answer here, so feel free to write the first thing that comes to mind.

What is for you the most challenging part of giving a presentation in front of a group of people?

_____

_____

READING

1 When asked about what abilities prove vital for success in life, people often think about things like intelligence, temperament, creativity, and even athleticism. One specific skill, however, often goes unmentioned: the ability to persuade others. The power of persuasion has helped certain individuals, for
5 instance, gather financiers to invest in the development of world-changing innovations, push entire populations to mobilize for war, inspire citizens to march for justice, and **motivate**[1] young people to pursue their dreams. While many traits and qualities can help explain what
10 enables someone to make a persuasive argument, the ancient Greek philosopher Aristotle outlined three key factors that seem just as relevant today as they were in his own lifetime over two thousand years ago: *ethos*, *pathos*, and *logos*, which are Greek words that in this context
15 translate as "character," "emotion," and "reason." While Aristotle's detailed analysis in his *Art of Rhetoric* focused primarily on giving a speech, which was the primary

Aristotle is one of the most influential philosophers in history, and his work is quite diverse, ranging from philosophy to biology.

mode of debate in ancient Greece, the principles that he outlines apply to making an argument in general, whether in written or spoken form. Let us therefore take a
20 closer look at these three factors in order to not only better understand how to make an effective argument, but in order to also recognize how others may try to use these specific techniques to persuade us.

2 The first key to persuading others, according to Aristotle, is by demonstrating good character, primarily in the form of credibility. In essence, it is important to
25 instill in others confidence about one's understanding of the matter being argued. This is of course much more easily accomplished if a speaker or writer is someone who has achieved world-renowned success, as is the case for people like Nobel laureates, notable celebrities, or high-ranking government officials. For instance, someone who has won the Nobel Peace Prize will have little difficulty establishing his or
30 her credibility when writing an op-ed or giving a speech about a topic relating to something like the importance of international agreements on arms control. Aristotle makes clear, however, that a preexisting **reputation**[2] is not necessary to make a persuasive argument. Instead, it is the way that someone presents himself or herself while making an argument that is most crucial to its effectiveness. This means that

world-renowned public figures can lose credibility by presenting themselves poorly while making an argument, while people who are completely unknown can raise their credibility by demonstrating that they have put careful analysis and preparation into their argument.

04 CD

3 The second key to the art of persuasion is having the ability to generate 5 an appropriate emotional response in one's audience, since for most people their emotional state affects their judgment. Successfully persuading others therefore entails knowing one's audience, Aristotle notes, and what type of emotional state will make that audience more likely to support the argument being made. If being in an angry state of mind, for example, is likely to make people more receptive to a 10 particular proposal, then finding a way to rile people up will likely make it easier to persuade them. This may explain why so many successful high-profile speeches and presentations today feature stories and anecdotes. Politicians campaigning for office, CEOs introducing new products, and keynote speakers at functions like graduation ceremonies, for instance, often spend a lot of time talking about things like their 15 own formative experiences, or an incident involving someone that they have met personally, in a way that connects to the theme of their presentation. One reason for this is that talking about a few specific incidents is oftentimes a more effective way to stimulate an emotional response than by presenting pure facts and statistics about the topic at hand. 20

05 CD

4 The third and final key to making a persuasive argument comes down to the argument itself. In essence, polishing one's delivery method and making one's audience emotionally receptive to an argument is important, but it is necessary to still make sure that the argument itself is strong. An argument must be logical, coherent, and feature sufficient proof to support the claims being made. Furthermore, brevity 25 is also important since an audience's time and attention span is limited. This means that writers and presenters should **eliminate**[3] any extraneous and banal information that does not support the argument being made.

06 CD

5 Aristotle's *Art of Rhetoric* has long served as a guide of sorts for aspiring orators and rhetoricians, but it is important to also view it in the context of his broader 30 philosophical work. His analysis of character, for example, partly aligns with his thoughts on aesthetics, while his analysis of emotion supports his rudimentary views on human psychology, and his focus on reason connects to his writings on logic. It is therefore in some ways better to see the *Art of Rhetoric* less as a guide for improving one's ability to persuade others, and instead view it more as an invaluable tool for 35 understanding the way that others use rhetoric to persuade us. When presented with a seemingly persuasive argument, it is therefore useful to recall Aristotle's analysis and ask ourselves a few basic questions. Does the way that someone is making his or her argument reveal good character traits, like credibility and reliability? What kind

5 of emotional response is someone's argument trying to evoke, and how is this emotional response affecting the listener's or reader's judgment? Finally, and perhaps most importantly, has the person provided adequate proof to support the claims

アリストテレスについて、
章末の Point of Interest を
読んでみよう。

made in his or her argument? These may seem like commonsensical questions, but they

10 are more important than ever as people today face a barrage of persuasion campaigns from what is effectively an endless stream of strangers, such as influencers on social media, advertisers online and on television, and social and political activists. In this way, then, even though it has been over two millennia since Aristotle formulated his analysis, it is clear that the lessons from his work on rhetoric remain relevant today.

NOTES

athleticism「運動能力」 **persuasion**「説得」 **financier**「財政家、大投資家」 **innovation**「新基軸」 **mobilize**「動員する」 **persuasive**「説得力のある」 **Aristotle**「アリストテレス (384−322b.c.)」 *Art of Rhetoric*「『弁論術』」 **credibility**「信頼性」 **instill**「しみ込ませる」 **laureate**「受賞者」 **celebrity**「著名人」 **op-ed**「(社説欄の向かい側の) 署名入り記事のページ」 **preexisting**「前から存在する」 **rile up**「激怒させる」 **high-profile**「卓越した」 **CEO**「最高経営責任者 (chief executive officer)」 **extraneous**「無関係の」 **banal**「陳腐な」 **align**「提携する」 **commonsensical**「常識的な」 **barrage**「多数」 **advertiser**「広告主」

▌ VOCABULARY

For each underlined word below, choose the option that most closely approximates its meaning based on the way that it is used in the reading section.

1. … and <u>motivate</u> young people to …
   a. inspire   **b.** persuade   **c.** frighten

2. … a preexisting <u>reputation</u> is not necessary …
   a. education   **b.** name   **c.** status

3. … presenters should <u>eliminate</u> any extraneous …
   a. highlight   **b.** remove   **c.** feature

COMPREHENSION QUESTIONS

Read each statement below carefully, and then based on the information presented in this chapter, write "T" if it is true or "F" if it is false.

1. _____ The three key traits that Aristotle outlines are *ethos*, *pathos*, and *logos*, which translate as "intelligence," "emotion," and "reason."

2. _____ In order for a speaker or writer to have strong credibility, it is necessary that he or she have noteworthy accomplishments.

3. _____ According to Aristotle, different emotional states of mind are receptive to different types of arguments.

4. _____ An argument should not only aim for coherence and proof that supports its claims, but it should also aim for brevity.

5. _____ The *Art of Rhetoric* does not fit in with the rest of Aristotle's work, which primarily focuses on philosophy.

PUTTING IT ALL TOGETHER

For each paragraph in the reading section, compose one complete sentence that summarizes the main theme of that paragraph.

Paragraph 1: _____

_____

Paragraph 2: _____

_____

Paragraph 3: _____

_____

Paragraph 4: _____

_____

Paragraph 5: _____

_____

Write a complete sentence that states whether your answer to the question below is "yes" or "no." Then write a sentence that provides support for your answer.

> Does the author argue that Aristotle's three key points are useful solely for enhancing one's own ability to make an effective argument?

_____

_____

_____

_____

① 07

POINT OF INTEREST

Listen carefully to the audio recording for this section and fill in the blanks in the paragraph below.

Ancient Athens produced what is 1.) _____ one of the most intellectually influential trio of thinkers in history, which began with Socrates and ended with Aristotle. Socrates was not a formally trained philosopher, and may well have been 2.) _____, but his teachings laid the foundations for Western philosophy. His most notable student, Plato, went on to become one of the most influential philosophers in the history of Western philosophy, and he 3.) _____ the Academy, an advanced school that was the precursor to modern elite academies. One of Plato's students, Aristotle, went on to become arguably the most influential intellectual 4.) _____ in European history until the Renaissance. Amazingly, many of Plato's and Aristotle's works have 5.) _____ and remain the subjects of academic inquiry and, as shown from this chapter's discussion on rhetoric, still hold value to this day.

COOL AS ICE

Can ice hockey become a truly global sport?

メジャーなプロのチーム・スポーツはたいてい、何らかのボールを使い、選手が
コートやフィールドを走るが、一つだけそれに当てはまらないスポーツがある。
アイスホッケーだ。アイスホッケーは、他のプロスポーツとどのような相違点や
類似点があるだろうか。また、将来的にアイスホッケーの人気はさらに上昇する
だろうか。

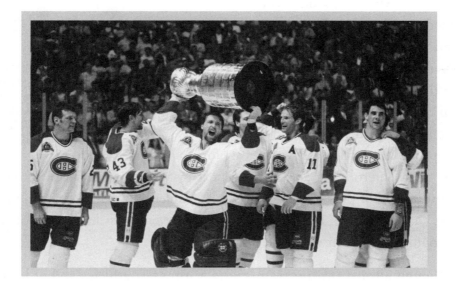

Patrick Roy, goaltender for the Montreal Canadiens at the time, is seen here
holding the Stanley Cup after his team won it in 1993.

▶ GETTING STARTED

*Think about the question below and then write a short response. There is no right or wrong
answer here, so feel free to write the first thing that comes to mind.*

What is your favorite sport to watch as a spectator, and what is the main reason why
you find it enjoyable to watch?

_____

_____

READING

1 Most mainstream professional team sports, such as baseball, rugby, soccer, basketball, and American football, use some type of ball and feature athletes running on some kind of field or court. One major team sport, however, is noticeably different: ice hockey. Hockey players skate

5 on ice, while using a hockey stick to pass and shoot a small hard rubber disc called a hockey puck. Each team starts with a lineup of six players on the ice, usually made up of three forwards who focus on scoring goals,

10 two defenders who focus on preventing their opponents from getting scoring chances, and a heavily padded goaltender who focuses on stopping the puck when the other team takes a shot on net. Although every sport can stake

15 a claim to being uniquely entertaining, hockey can perhaps make a particularly strong case for

Superstar forward Auston Matthews was born in California and grew up in Arizona, and became one of the best players in the NHL, making him a great example of the league's successful expansion into non-traditional markets.

being the most entertaining and unique sport by virtue of the speed of the game and the **intensity**[1] of play on the ice. As this chapter will demonstrate, despite the challenges that come with this sport, ice hockey nevertheless has great potential to

20 grow in popularity in years to come.

2 Though all mainstream team sports feature fast athletes and at least some moments of intense physical play, hockey is perhaps the fastest and most physical. Since each team typically scores only a few goals per game, most goals have the potential to be **decisive**[2] in any game's outcome. Players therefore skate at full speed

25 toward their opponent's net on a scoring opportunity and race back to their end of the ice to play defense, and they even sacrifice their bodies by blocking blistering slapshots that can go over a hundred miles per hour. The game often gets quite physical, with players frequently bodychecking one another into the boards. This kind of intensity leads to frequent pushing and shoving after a stoppage in play, and

30 can even lead to full-fledged fist fights when the tension finally boils over.

3 Professional hockey leagues are found predominantly in Canada, the United States, Russia, Sweden, Finland, and other European countries, but when fans want to watch the best of the best, they look to the National Hockey League (NHL). This league, which features the very best players in the world, has grown dramatically since its inception in the early twentieth century. In 1966 there were only six teams, all concentrated in eastern North America near the Canada-U.S. border. The league has steadily expanded numerically since then, and with the most recent addition of a team in Las Vegas in 2017 and in Seattle in 2021, thirty-two teams now comprise the NHL—seven based in Canadian cities and twenty-five based in American cities. ₅ The league has also expanded geographically by not only adding new teams to other parts of North America, but also by relocating some existing teams, such as: the Québec Nordiques, renamed the Avalanche upon moving to Colorado in 1995; the Winnipeg Jets, renamed the Coyotes upon moving to Arizona in 1996; and the Hartford Whalers, renamed the Hurricanes upon moving to North Carolina in 1997. ₁₀

11 🎧

4 Throughout much of the NHL's history, well over half of the league's players were Canadian. There are now still more players from Canada than from any other country, but the number of Canadian players as a percentage of the league's rosters has been steadily decreasing. More than half of NHL players today come from a combination of other countries, most notably the United States, Sweden, Russia, ₁₅ the Czech Republic, Finland, and a few others. Given Canada's dominance in the sport, it is perhaps fitting that it is a team named the "Canadiens" that is the winningest franchise in NHL history. The Canadiens franchise, located in the city of Montréal, Québec, has won the Stanley Cup, which is the NHL's championship trophy, twenty-three times since the league was formed in ₂₀ 1917. By way of comparison, the second winningest franchise in NHL history has won it only thirteen times. The storied Montréal franchise is one of the original six teams from the time before the NHL began to expand in 1967, and this team has featured some of the league's most iconic stars, like Maurice "The Rocket" ₂₅ Richard, a famously fast and fiery player, and Guy Lafleur, a prolific goal-scorer who led the Canadiens to four consecutive Stanley Cup victories in the late 1970s. Despite the franchise's impressive history of Stanley Cup success, however, the team has not won a championship since 1993.

前回のカナディアンズのスタンレーカップ優勝について、章末の Point of Interest を読んでみよう。

12 🎧

5 Professional hockey is in many ways a microcosm of professional sports in ₃₀ general, insofar as it faces issues that are also prevalent in other professional sports leagues. The risk of head injuries, for instance, has become a growing concern in contact sports in light of revelations that repeated concussions can lead to chronic traumatic encephalopathy (CTE). Some of the NHL's biggest stars have in the past suffered severe head injuries, and so the league has had to develop concussion protocols ₃₅ and enact stricter disciplinary measures to protect players. As with other major professional sports leagues in North America, the billions of dollars in revenue can lead to acrimonious negotiations between players and owners over salaries. Anytime a collective bargaining agreement between a pro sports league and the association representing the players nears expiration, the prospect of a work stoppage looms large.

5 In the case of the NHL, some disagreements have been so **substantial**[3] that player strikes have resulted in some seasons starting late, or even getting canceled entirely, as was the case with the 2004-2005 season. Finally, as with other North American sports leagues, the NHL seeks to expand its brand and grow its audience, both within North America and more broadly throughout other parts of the world. Hockey faces

10 a unique challenge given that ice arenas are cost-prohibitive in many parts of the world, but given the NHL's success thus far in expanding to non-traditional markets in the United States, it is clear that ice hockey has the potential to grow even more popular in the coming decades.

NOTES

noticeably「目立って」 **goaltender**「ゴールキーパー」 **stake a claim**「権利を主張する」 **blistering**「強烈な」 **slapshot**「スラップショット（フルスイングで放つ強力なシュート）」 **full-fledged**「徹底した」 **predominantly**「主として」 **inception**「発足」 **concentrated**「集中する」 **roster**「登録選手名簿」 **winningest**「最多勝利の」 **franchise**「加盟チーム」 **storied**「歴史に名高い」 **iconic**「代表的な」 **Maurice Richard**「モーリス・リシャール (1921 – 2000)」 **Guy Lafleur**「ギイ・ラフレール (1951 – 2022)」 **consecutive**「連続する」 **microcosm**「縮図」 **prevalent**「一般的な」 **revelation**「意外な新事実」 **concussion**「脳震とう」 **chronic traumatic encephalopathy**「慢性外傷性脳症」 **acrimonious**「激しい」 **collective bargaining agreement**「団体労働協約」 **expiration**「終了」 **work stoppage**「ストライキ」 **cost-prohibitive**「膨大なコストがかかる」

◀ VOCABULARY

For each underlined word below, choose the option that most closely approximates its meaning based on the way that it is used in the reading section.

1. … speed of the game and the <u>intensity</u> of play …
   a. forcefulness   **b.** swiftness   **c.** honesty

2. … the potential to be <u>decisive</u> in any game's …
   a. critical   **b.** decision-making   **c.** truthful

3. … been so <u>substantial</u> that player strikes have …
   a. fleeting   **b.** interesting   **c.** considerable

COMPREHENSION QUESTIONS

Read each statement below carefully, and then based on the information presented in this chapter, write "T" if it is true or "F" if it is false.

1. _____ Goaltenders are heavily padded players who are responsible for preventing the opposing team from getting scoring chances.

2. _____ Hockey is a fast sport that features slapshots that can go over a hundred miles per hour.

3. _____ The National Hockey League grew from six teams in 1966 to thirty-two teams in 2021.

4. _____ Today there are players in the NHL from various countries, but more than half of all players come from Canada.

5. _____ A big concern for hockey players is chronic traumatic encephalopathy, which is a serious injury to ligaments in the knee.

PUTTING IT ALL TOGETHER

For each paragraph in the reading section, compose one complete sentence that summarizes the main theme of that paragraph.

Paragraph 1: _____

_____

Paragraph 2: _____

_____

Paragraph 3: _____

_____

Paragraph 4: _____

_____

Paragraph 5: _____

_____

Write a complete sentence that states whether your answer to the question below is "yes" or "no." Then write a sentence that provides support for your answer.

> Hockey is a unique mainstream team sport since it is played on ice, but does this mean that it has nothing in common with other sports?

① 13 **CD**

POINT OF INTEREST

Listen carefully to the audio recording for this section and fill in the blanks in the paragraph below.

In 1988, Wayne Gretzky was known as "The Great One" and was almost 1.) _____ acclaimed as the greatest hockey player ever. He won the Stanley Cup for the 2.) _____ time with the Edmonton Oilers, but was then shockingly traded to the Los Angeles Kings. The Kings made it to the Stanley Cup finals five years later, setting up a 3.) _____ series that featured Gretzky, virtually undisputed as the sport's greatest offensive player of all time, against the Montreal Canadiens, led by the player now widely regarded as one of the greatest goaltenders of all time—Patrick Roy. The Canadiens won the best-of-seven series four games to one, making the team the 1993 Stanley Cup 4.) _____, and for Roy it was his second Stanley Cup and his second Conn Smythe Trophy, which is awarded to the best player in the playoffs. Roy would go on to win two more Stanley Cups with 5.) _____ team, and in 2001 he became the only player ever to win the Conn Smythe a third time, while unfortunately for Gretzky, he never again reached the Stanley Cup finals.

CANCEL CULTURE

Is it time to reconsider the limits of free speech?

自分自身の考えを、処罰されるかもしれないという恐れを持たずに自由に表現できる権利は、現代の自由民主主義の社会の根幹である。しかしこの数十年の間に、世の中は大きく変化した。中でも注目すべきは、多くの人に自分の考えを広めることができるソーシャルメディアの出現だ。時にはフェイク・ニュースやヘイト・スピーチといった有害なメッセージも拡散される。表現の自由の制限を再考する時がきたのだろうか。

Many were stunned in 2022 when one of the richest men in the world, Elon Musk, bought Twitter. Part of the reason for Musk's expressed interest in acquiring Twitter was due to his desire to loosen the social media platform's content moderation policies and thereby protect free speech.

▶ GETTING STARTED

Think about the question below and then write a short response. There is no right or wrong answer here, so feel free to write the first thing that comes to mind.

Has your experience on social media, either from uploading content or viewing content, been generally positive, or largely negative?

_____

_____

READING

14

1 The right to express oneself freely stands as a core principle in modern democratic societies. The rise of social media, however, has allowed people to post videos and written comments online that sometimes push the boundaries of legally protected expression, which has sparked intense debate over how far free speech can go. Some argue that socially undesirable speech should be restricted online, given that the leading social media platforms host hundreds of millions of interconnected users, and given that much of the content posted is so easily accessible and hard to completely remove once it is disseminated online. Others argue that stifling free expression is fueling cancel culture, whereby people seek to silence those with whom they disagree. There have always been restrictions on speech, such as prohibitions against inciting violence or making false and defamatory statements, but as we will see in this chapter, the rise of social media has led some to question whether or not the traditional free speech defenses still apply today.

15

2 Although hardly a free society by today's standards, ancient Athens is widely regarded as the birthplace of democracy. The city's democratic form of decision-making, along with its open discussions that frequently included criticism of the city's rulers and their decisions, made Athens uniquely free by the standards of the day. One oppressive act in particular, though, would go on to live in infamy and serve as one of the most profoundly inspirational events for free speech advocates for generations to come. The philosopher Socrates questioned everyone and everything in the pursuit of truth, and he encouraged his students to do the same. When he asked some of the city's most powerful figures basic philosophical questions, they often answered in ways that **exposed**[1] their ignorance. The resulting embarrassment they experienced generated resentment against Socrates, and so some of these influential men ultimately managed to have him put on trial in 399 BCE for impiety and for corrupting the youth.

This iconic eighteenth-century painting by French artist Jacques Louis David portrays Socrates as he is about to drink poison, in fulfilment of his death sentence.

According to Plato's account of the trial, after the jury voted and declared him guilty, Socrates had an opportunity to ask for leniency. However, rather than ask for leniency, he instead declared that his approach of questioning everything in the pursuit of truth should be rewarded rather than punished. This brash stance resulted in Socrates being sentenced to death, which he faced courageously and defiantly, even declining an opportunity to escape before the death penalty could be carried out.

16 🎧

3 This unwillingness to give up asking questions, even in the face of death, inspired many relatively recent free speech advocates. An eighteenth-century French 5 philosopher named François-Marie Arouet, who took the penname Voltaire, was clearly inspired by the defiance that Socrates exhibited, and he even went so far as to write a play titled *Socrates*, which re-enacts some of the events near the end of the ancient Athenian philosopher's life. Voltaire ended up suffering a fate similar to what Socrates experienced, for he ended up being imprisoned in one of France's 10 harshest prisons for offending the king's regent. Upon his release, Voltaire remained defiant and went on to publish several works that helped inspire some of the leading figures of the American Revolution and the French Revolution.

> アメリカ革命について、
> 章末の Point of Interest
> を読んでみよう。

His writings covered a wide range of subjects, but many of them focused on the 15 importance of personal freedoms, including the freedom to express oneself. One of the most frequently cited quotes in defense of free speech today is one typically attributed to him: "I disapprove of what you say, but will defend to the death your right to say it." Although there is no evidence that he ever wrote or spoke these exact words, this bold statement reflects his general message about the importance of 20 allowing everyone to express themselves freely.

17 🎧

4 One of the leading thinkers of the nineteenth century, British political philosopher John Stuart Mill, also referenced the **execution**[2] of Socrates while making an argument about the importance of free speech. In his most famous work, *On Liberty*, Mill suggests that a large group of people silencing one person 25 is as unjustifiable as when one person silences a large group of people. It is just as inappropriate, in other words, for a democratic society to silence an unpopular opinion held by just one person as it is for a dictator to silence an entire society. To support his argument, Mill notes that "all silencing of discussion is an **assumption**[3] of infallibility." His point is that silencing someone with whom we disagree runs the 30 risk of silencing someone who may actually be correct.

18 🎧

5 Times have obviously changed dramatically since Voltaire and Mill made their passionate defenses of free speech. Disseminating messages to large audiences in the past typically required going through broadcasters and publishers. This approach limits who can reach a large audience, and also what someone can write or say since 35

editors and lawyers typically scrutinize any content disseminated to the public. Debates about free speech have thus long focused primarily on specific incidents involving newspapers, publishers, high-profile public figures, and government regulations on speech. The rapid growth of social media, however, has seemingly
5 made the issue of free speech an ongoing and universal debate since just about anyone can now disseminate messages to a large audience. The problem is that, on the one hand, unfettered free speech has the potential to create a toxic atmosphere on social media platforms that may also spill over into daily life. Individuals in some cases can spread hate speech, malicious rumors, fake news, and exhibit a general lack of
10 civility. In effect, the apparent anonymity that social media confers on many of its users makes it possible for some of the worst human impulses to flourish. Seen in this way, it seems as though the classic defense of free speech is outdated. On the other hand, having the government and social media platforms regulate speech runs the risk of granting those in positions of authority the ability to shape public discourse
15 in ways that benefit their own interests. Seen in this way, this latter prospect seems to reinforce classic arguments about the importance of free speech. Either way, free speech in the social media era is clearly a complex issue that will surely remain the subject of intense debate for the foreseeable future.

NOTES

disseminate「広める」 **stifle**「抑圧する」 **fuel**「あおる」 **cancel culture**「キャンセル・カルチャー（主にソーシャルメディア上で人物が言動などを理由に追放される排斥の形態）」 **defamatory**「中傷的な」 **oppressive**「弾圧的な」 **infamy**「不名誉、汚名」 **profoundly**「非常に」 **inspirational**「鼓舞する」 **Socrates**「ソクラテス (c.470 – 399 b.c.)」 **embarrassment**「気恥ずかしさ」 **BCE**「Before the Common Era の略記で、b.c.（紀元前）に対応する非キリスト教徒の用語」 **impiety**「不敬な行為」 **corrupt**「堕落させる」 **leniency**「寛大な判決」 **brash**「豪胆な」 **defiantly**「挑戦的に、反抗的に」 **François-Marie Arouet**「フランソワ＝マリ・アルーエ (1694 – 1778)」 **Voltaire**「ヴォルテール (1694 – 1778)」 **re-enact**「再現する」 **harsh**「厳しい」 **regent**「摂政」 **quote**「引用文」 **John Stuart Mill**「ジョン・スチュアート・ミル (1806–73)」 *On Liberty*「『自由論』」 **silence**「口を封じる」 **infallibility**「不過誤」 **scrutinize**「吟味する」 **unfettered**「制限されていない」 **toxic**「有害な」 **civility**「礼儀正しさ」 **anonymity**「匿名」 **impulse**「衝動」 **reinforce**「補強する」 **for the foreseeable future**「当面は」

◤ VOCABULARY

For each underlined word below, choose the option that most closely approximates its meaning based on the way that it is used in the reading section.

1. … answered in ways that <u>exposed</u> their …
    a. reduced   **b.** revealed   **c.** increased

2. … referenced the <u>execution</u> of Socrates …
    a. death   **b.** exile   **c.** defeat

3. … silencing of discussion is an <u>assumption</u> of …
    a. belief   **b.** guess   **c.** failing

COMPREHENSION QUESTIONS

Read each statement below carefully, and then based on the information presented in this chapter, write "T" if it is true or "F" if it is false.

1. _____ The expression "cancel culture" refers to people trying to silence others with whom they disagree.

2. _____ Socrates ended up being put on trial because he and his students drew the ire of powerful men in Athens.

3. _____ Voltaire famously wrote: "I disapprove of what you say, but will defend to the death your right to say it."

4. _____ According to Mill, the worst violation of free speech is when a dictator silences an entire society.

5. _____ Some of the worst human impulses flourish on social media due to being able to remain anonymous online.

PUTTING IT ALL TOGETHER

For each paragraph in the reading section, compose one complete sentence that summarizes the main theme of that paragraph.

Paragraph 1: _____

_____

Paragraph 2: _____

_____

Paragraph 3: _____

_____

Paragraph 4: _____

_____

Paragraph 5: _____

_____

Write a complete sentence that states whether your answer to the question below is "yes" or "no." Then write a sentence that provides support for your answer.

> Since there was no form of social media during Mill's time, or in Voltaire's day, are their free speech arguments now irrelevant today?

_____

_____

_____

_____

① 19 CD

POINT OF INTEREST

Listen carefully to the audio recording for this section and fill in the blanks in the paragraph below.

After winning independence from Britain in the Revolutionary War, the thirteen newly independent American 1.) _____ engaged in debate about a proposed constitution that would unite them into one country. Some Americans at the time, however, feared that the new proposed government could end up 2.) _____ too powerful and tyrannical. To alleviate these fears, the chief architect of the Constitution of the United States, James Madison, 3.) _____ ten amendments, collectively known as the Bill of Rights. The very first amendment guarantees that the government will not create any law that 4.) _____ people from freely expressing themselves, and also guarantees freedom of the press, the freedom of religion, and the freedom to peacefully protest. Many other countries that have 5.) _____ since then feature similar constitutional provisions that protect individual freedom of expression to varying degrees.

NINTENDO POWER

How did video games become so popular?

世界中でゲーム産業が栄えている現代では想像しがたいかもしれないが、1980年代初期のアメリカ合衆国では、ゲーム業界には未来がないと思われていた。何がその窮地を救うきっかけとなったのか。またその後ゲームによって、良きにつけ悪しきにつけどのような影響がもたらされたのか。

Video game arcades, like the one pictured here, were immensely popular from the late seventies until their appeal began to decline in the late nineties, due in large part to the growth of the home video game industry.

▶ GETTING STARTED

Think about the question below and then write a short response. There is no right or wrong answer here, so feel free to write the first thing that comes to mind.

In comparison with other types of games, from sports to board games, how interested are you in playing video games?

_____

_____

READING

1 Video games are today among the most popular forms of entertainment, and they have grown into a major economic force that rivals other leading industries. Not so long ago, however, the notion of home video games as a major industry appeared rather farfetched, particularly in the United States, due to what is known

5 as the video game crash of 1983. At the time, home gaming consoles had quickly fallen out of favor with American consumers and the video game industry appeared ready to fade away, but the emergence of Nintendo, a Japanese company that was virtually unknown to the American public, would change all of that. Let us therefore take a look at how the video game market **collapsed**[1] in the United States and how

10 Nintendo helped revive the seemingly doomed industry—and how this ultimately set gaming consoles on the path to becoming so common in households today, with all of the advantages and disadvantages that modern gaming entails.

2 Video games had relatively little appeal in the early seventies, but that all changed when gaming took a massive leap forward by the end of the decade. Arcade

15 games came to feature more **sophisticated**[2] graphics, and titles like the 1978 hit *Space Invaders*, the 1979 hit *Asteroids*, and especially the 1980 mega-hit *Pac-Man*, helped propel gaming into the mainstream. Home gaming consoles likewise started out in the early seventies as being dull, with a very limited selection of built-in games. Home video games blossomed at the end of the decade, with the Atari Video

20 Computer System, later renamed the Atari 2600, leading the way. As one of the very first consoles to play video game cartridges, this new gaming console revolutionized the home gaming industry by allowing owners to buy various games and continually grow their game collection as new titles came out. Atari's success was rather short-lived, though, for home video games experienced a marked decline in sales in 1983,

25 leading to the aforementioned video game market crash. Multiple reasons can help explain why the video game market crashed, but ultimately it largely came down to two factors. First, the proliferation of competing consoles resulted in supply vastly outstripping demand. Second, and perhaps most notably, various software manufacturers were releasing numerous low-quality games, many of which were

30 filled with glitches and unclear objectives.

3 Many market analysts at the time believed that the home gaming market was all but wiped out in the United States, but a new gaming console by Nintendo quickly reversed the industry's fortunes. Nintendo made some changes to its popular Family Computer, simply referred to as the Famicom in Japan, and released it in the United

States in 1985 as the Nintendo Entertainment System, usually simply called the NES. This console had a sleek design, easy-to-use controllers, and most importantly, it had what was at the time revolutionary sound and graphics capabilities. Nintendo also offered consumers a wide variety of quality games to play on its console, including two that have spawned franchises that to this day maintain a huge fan base: *Super* 5 *Mario Bros.* and *The Legend of Zelda*. The NES took the country by storm, and Nintendo became essentially synonymous with home video games in America, and around the world for that matter.

23 CD

4 Nintendo enjoyed largely unrivaled success in America until 1989, when a rival manufacturer, Sega, released a console called the Genesis. This sixteen-bit 10 console was considerably more powerful than the eight-bit NES. Moreover, Sega launched a game with a title character that could compete with Nintendo's famous Super Mario. Sega's Sonic the Hedgehog was charismatic and edgy, and offered a cool new approach to the side-scrolling adventure games that were so pervasive at the time. Several other companies also launched sixteen-bit consoles, but none could truly challenge the Sega Genesis in the American market—until Nintendo struck back with its own sixteen-bit console. Nintendo's second-generation console, the Super Nintendo Entertainment System, commonly known as the SNES, reaffirmed Nintendo's place as a dominant force in the gaming industry. This rivalry marked the beginning of what has been colloquially referred to as the console wars. The

Shigeru Miyamoto, seen here playing *Super Mario World* on the SNES, is responsible for Nintendo's iconic Mario franchise.

console wars primarily involved Nintendo and Sega in the first half of the nineties, but eventually grew to involve corporate giants Sony, which released the PlayStation in 1995, and Microsoft, which released the Xbox in 2001. Sega ultimately exited the console market the same year as the Microsoft console's release, which set up a three-way competition that still defines the game console industry to this day. 30

24 CD

5 Ultimately, it appears that Nintendo not only helped revive the American gaming industry by creating market demand for its NES console, but also by setting the bar so high for gaming consoles that other manufacturers had to push themselves hard to succeed. Nintendo also helped fuel the growth of the video game industry globally by getting video games entrenched in the world's largest 35 market. While there is no denying that video games are immensely entertaining and enjoyable for countless gamers around the world, games have become so realistic, so immersive, and feature themes so **diverse**[3] that some serious concerns arise when it comes to the effects that some games have on people, especially younger players. Online gaming, for instance, presents opportunities to play with strangers from

5　all around the world, which can expose players to verbal and text-based profanity and harassment. Another issue is the growth of violence in gaming, in the form of first-person shooters that simulate warlike environments and open-world games that allow players to simulate acts of violence in ordinary urban settings. The home gaming

10　industry, to put it simply, has changed dramatically since the early days when Nintendo first came on the scene. With three core console manufacturers and multiple powerhouse gaming software companies now continually pushing technological and, at times, societal boundaries, future innovations in hardware and software capabilities will likely remain coupled with

15　potentially adverse social effects.

昔のゲームが現代でも未だに人気があることについて、章末の Point of Interest を読んでみよう。

NOTES

farfetched「ありえない」　**crash**「暴落」　**entail**「伴う」　*Space Invaders*「『スペースインベーダー』」 *Asteroids*「『アステロイド』」　*Pac-Man*「『パックマン』」　**revolutionize**「一大進歩をもたらす」　**aforementioned**「前述の」　**proliferation**「急増」　**vastly**「非常に」　**outstrip**「上回る」　**glitch**「誤作動」　**fortunes**「命運、盛衰」　**sleek**「格好のいい」　**spawn**「生じさせる」　*Super Mario Bros.*「『スーパーマリオブラザーズ』」　*The Legend of Zelda*「『ゼルダの伝説』」　**synonymous**「同義語の」　Sonic the Hedgehog「ソニック・ザ・ヘッジホッグ」　**charismatic**「カリスマ性を持った」　**edgy**「斬新な」　**pervasive**「普及した」　**colloquially**「日常の会話では」　**corporate giant**「巨大企業」　**exit**「出て行く」　**three-way**「3社間の」　**entrench**「確立する」　**immersive**「ユーザーを包み込むような臨場感がある」　**first-person-shooter**「一人称シューティング（一人称視点で操作するタイプのシューティング・ゲーム）」

◀ VOCABULARY

For each underlined word below, choose the option that most closely approximates its meaning based on the way that it is used in the reading section.

1. … the video game market <u>collapsed</u> in the …
   a. drifted　　　　**b.** straightened　　　**c.** failed

2. … to feature more <u>sophisticated</u> graphics …
   a. high-quality　**b.** high-class　　　**c.** high-value

3. … themes so <u>diverse</u> that some serious …
   a. multicultural　**b.** varied　　　　**c.** distinct

◀ COMPREHENSION QUESTIONS

Read each statement below carefully, and then based on the information presented in this chapter, write "T" if it is true or "F" if it is false.

1. _____ Home video games appeared set to become a major industry in the United States in 1983.

2. _____ The Atari 2600, which was later renamed the Atari Video Computer System, was one of the first consoles to play video game cartridges.

3. _____ The NES did not offer a wide variety of games, but Mario and Zelda games attained a huge fan base.

4. _____ Nintendo's SNES could not compete with the Genesis, and so Sega took over as the dominant force in the gaming industry.

5. _____ Gaming has become an important social issue due to online interaction and the violent content in some games.

◀ PUTTING IT ALL TOGETHER

For each paragraph in the reading section, compose one complete sentence that summarizes the main theme of that paragraph.

Paragraph 1: _____

_____

Paragraph 2: _____

_____

Paragraph 3: _____

_____

Paragraph 4: _____

_____

Paragraph 5: _____

_____

Write a complete sentence that states whether your answer to the question below is "yes" or "no." Then write a sentence that provides support for your answer.

> Since Sega, Sony, and Microsoft eventually released their own consoles, does this mean that Nintendo was not that important in gaming history?

_____

_____

_____

_____

① 25 💿

◀ **POINT OF INTEREST**

Listen carefully to the audio recording for this section and fill in the blanks in the paragraph below.

Two examples highlight just how popular classic games have 1.) _____ in recent years. In 2016, for instance, Nintendo released the NES Classic Edition, which was a miniaturized 2.) _____ of the NES with thirty pre-installed classic NES games. The system was so popular that it was frequently sold out at most retailers, leading consumers to pay 3.) _____ more than the retail price on online auction sites like eBay in the United States. A similar situation 4.) _____ the following year when Nintendo released the Super NES Classic Edition, which featured twenty-one pre-installed classic SNES games. Further highlighting the popularity of classic video games is the way that some games that are still factory-sealed and in mint condition can fetch thousands of dollars, as was the case in 2021 when an 5.) _____ copy of the original *Super Mario Bros*. NES game, in perfect condition, sold for 660,000 U.S. dollars.

STRIVING FOR GREATNESS

What makes someone the greatest of all time?

過去から現在に至るまで、人間は自分が偉大であると主張したがるようだ。歴史
上のリーダーであるアレキサンダー大王のように自分の名前に偉大さを示す「大」
という文字（英語では Great という単語）を添えることもあれば、現代では、あ
るスポーツで誰が最優秀選手か、あるいはどれが最高傑作の映画かといった議論
がなされる。誰か、あるいは何かが、最も偉大であると言うとき、それは何を意
味するのだろうか。また客観的に誰（何）がもっとも偉大だと決めることは可能
なのだろうか。

Napoleon Bonaparte is widely considered one of the greatest military leaders
of all time. His legacy in France is complicated, but he is undoubtedly one of
the country's most notable historical figures, and so his tomb today remains
prominently on display in Paris.

GETTING STARTED

*Think about the question below and then write a short response. There is no right or wrong
answer here, so feel free to write the first thing that comes to mind.*

In your opinion, who is the greatest public figure, such as a sports star or a politician,
in Japanese history?

_____

_____

READING

1 Many people throughout history have staked a claim to greatness. The list of greats in history is long and distinguished, and just to name a few, includes ancient Persian ruler Darius the Great, Roman emperor Constantine the Great, Macedonian conqueror Alexander the Great, Russian tsar Peter the Great, Russian
5 empress Catherine the Great, and King of the Franks and the first Holy Roman Emperor Charlemagne, a French name that literally translates as Charles the Great. As this brief list of historical figures makes evident, claims to greatness date back millennia. Today, discussions about greatness often focus on who or what is the greatest in a particular category, such as, historical figures, sports stars, movie
10 directors, and video game titles. In fact, a quick search online for a particular topic will often yield multiple blogs and vlogs that feature lists of the top five or the top ten greatest for that particular topic, such as the top ten greatest movies of all time. A closer look at the concept of greatness and specific claims of someone or something being the greatest, however, reveals just how difficult it is to support
15 such claims.

2 When it comes to greatness, the concept itself is inherently subjective. Whether in reference to size or in reference to accomplishments, it is not possible to precisely measure greatness. When it comes to size, it is indisputable that the
20 Great Pyramid of Giza, for instance, is great relative to the other pyramids in the Giza pyramid complex. On the other hand, if someone were to propose building a great structure, without specifying other
25 structures for the sake of comparison, then it would be difficult to get a sense of the proposed building's size. The same line of argument applies when discussing achievements and accomplishments, for it

The Great Pyramid of Giza is the tallest and clearly stands out from the others in the Giza pyramid complex.

30 is sensible to describe one athlete or military leader as great in relation to others when based on a specific metric, such as victories, but it would be purely subjective to categorize someone as the greatest athlete or military leader without specific facts that elevate him or her above his or her peers.

28 CD

3 Even when facts and statistics offer a **straightforward**[1] way to make comparisons, proving that someone or something is the greatest is still challenging. For instance, greatness is a common topic in discussions relating to professional sports. While there is relatively little debate when it comes to describing some of the most successful athletes of a given sport as being "among the greatest of all 5 time," intense debate does arise when it comes to labeling someone as "the greatest of all time," a phrase that is often colloquially abbreviated as "the GOAT." In American football, for instance, Tom Brady is widely regarded as the GOAT, and for good reason. He has won more Super Bowls, which is the National Football League's annual championship game, than any other player, and he sits atop 10 virtually every significant statistical category for quarterbacks. It is therefore easy to proclaim him the greatest quarterback to ever play—in terms of statistics. Some fans and observers, however, would argue that it is not enough to measure greatness in football in purely statistical terms. For instance, the nature of the game and the rules have changed over the years in ways that have given quarterbacks of Brady's 15 era immense advantages in comparison with the conditions in which quarterbacks of previous generations had to play. Furthermore, given that football is a team sport, it is difficult to determine precisely how much of a quarterback's success is a **product**[2] of his own abilities as opposed to the quality of his teammates and coaches. 20

29 CD

4 Similar discussions arise with history's most successful military leaders, such as Alexander the Great, Julius Caesar, Genghis Khan, and Napoleon Bonaparte. Debates about which of these men was the most successful conqueror focus on comparing their military successes and their particular circumstances. In the late fourth century BCE, for instance, Alexander the Great led his troops to 25 victory against overwhelming odds on multiple occasions and forged a massive empire in the process. By way of comparison, Napoleon Bonaparte helped pull France out of the chaos it was experiencing during the French Revolution, and he subsequently led the French army to victory on 30 numerous occasions, giving France control over much of continental Europe in the early nineteenth century. It is difficult to declare one of these leaders the greatest ever, for they lived in different time periods and faced different circumstances. Moreover, some argue that to even use the term "great" for men who were willing to spill so much blood to satisfy their ambitions is inappropriate given this term's 35 positive connotations.

ナポレオンについて、章末の Point of Interest を読んでみよう。

5 Ultimately, then, what constitutes greatness is obviously a matter of opinion, but clearly not in a purely subjective way as is the case when someone merely expresses a **preference**[3] for one thing over something else. To assess someone or something as great, or even the greatest, represents a claim that someone's or something's qualities stand out as significantly above average in a measurable way. This does not mean that greatness can be fully measured objectively, for as this chapter has shown, too many variables are at play to make perfectly objective comparisons possible when evaluating greatness. It therefore seems pointless to declare anyone the greatest ever in any particular field, but such discussions serve as ideal topics to spur debate and analysis, and they also set the bar for others who strive for greatness.

NOTES

Darius the Great「ダレイオス大王 (550 – 486b.c.)」　**Constantine the Great**「コンスタンティヌス大帝 (280 – 337)」　**Alexander the Great**「アレキサンダー大王 (356 – 323b.c.)」　**Peter the Great**「ピョートル大帝 (1672 – 1725)」　**Catherine the Great**「エカチェリーナ女帝 (1729 – 96)」　**Holy Roman Emperor Charlemagne**「シャルルマーニュ神聖ローマ皇帝 (742 – 814)」　**vlog**「ビデオブログ」　**inherently**「本質的に」　**accomplishment**「成果、業績」　**indisputable**「議論の余地のない」　**pyramid complex**「ピラミッド群」　**metric**「測定基準」　**abbreviate**「略す」　**Tom Brady**「トム・ブレイディ (1977–)」　**proclaim**「宣する」　**Julius Caesar**「ユリウス・カエサル (Gaius Julius Caesar 100–44b.c.)」　**Genghis Khan**「ジンギスカン (c.1162–1227)」　**Napoleon Bonaparte**「ナポレオン・ボナパルト (1769–1821)」　**overwhelming**「圧倒的な」　**odds**「勝ち目」　**forge**「築く」　**connotation**「(言外の) 意味」

▶ VOCABULARY

For each underlined word below, choose the option that most closely approximates its meaning based on the way that it is used in the reading section.

1. … statistics offer a <u>straightforward</u> way to …
   a. clear　　**b.** blunt　　**c.** front-facing

2. … success is a <u>product</u> of his own abilities …
   a. item　　**b.** creation　　**c.** result

3. … expresses a <u>preference</u> for one thing …
   a. certainty　　**b.** liking　　**c.** habit

COMPREHENSION QUESTIONS

Read each statement below carefully, and then based on the information presented in this chapter, write "T" if it is true or "F" if it is false.

1. _____ The list of historical figures with "the Great" in their name includes Alexander, Darius, Catherine, and Peter.

2. _____ The Great Pyramid of Giza is indisputably the greatest, in terms of size, in relation to the other pyramids in the Giza pyramid complex.

3. _____ Tom Brady is the leader in most of the NFL's quarterback stats, but this does not necessarily prove that he is the greatest quarterback ever.

4. _____ The term "great" is perhaps inappropriate when referring to successful military leaders due to the bloodshed they caused.

5. _____ What constitutes greatness is a purely subjective matter that reflects personal preferences.

PUTTING IT ALL TOGETHER

For each paragraph in the reading section, compose one complete sentence that summarizes the main theme of that paragraph.

Paragraph 1: _____

_____

Paragraph 2: _____

_____

Paragraph 3: _____

_____

Paragraph 4: _____

_____

Paragraph 5: _____

_____

DEBATING THE ISSUES

Write a complete sentence that states whether your answer to the question below is "yes" or "no." Then write a sentence that provides support for your answer.

> If facts and statistics are used to compare certain people to one another in a particular vocation, is it possible to determine who is the greatest?

_____

_____

_____

_____

① 31 CD

POINT OF INTEREST

Listen carefully to the audio recording for this section and fill in the blanks in the paragraph below.

Napoleon is widely **1.)** _____ as one of the greatest military leaders of all time, for his military conquests made France the master of continental Europe for the duration of his reign as emperor. Though his victories vastly outnumber his defeats, it is one of these **2.)** _____ defeats that stands out as his most famous battle: Waterloo. Following France's defeat at the hands of a grand European alliance and Napoleon's subsequent exile to the small Mediterranean island of Elba, the **3.)** _____ emperor returned to France the following year. European armies quickly mobilized, led most **4.)** _____ by Britain's Duke of Wellington, and squared off against Napoleon at Waterloo, Belgium, on June 18, 1815. Napoleon made a few critical mistakes while preparing for battle and during the battle itself, and in combination with French forces being outnumbered, his bid to return to power ended in failure and exile—this time to St. Helena, a remote island in the south Atlantic, where he **5.)** _____ until his death in 1821.

AS THE WORLD BURNS

What is fueling wildfires around the globe?

竜巻や地震、台風などのあらゆる自然災害は、大きな被害をもたらす可能性があり、人命が失われることもある。しかし、ある自然災害は、これまであまり注目されてこなかった。山火事である。山火事は火が広がると壊滅的な被害もたらす。なぜ山火事は起こるのか、また未然に防ぐにはどうしたらよいのか。

Wildfires wreak havoc wherever they spread, and even with the help of aerial support the best firefighters sometimes struggle to contain them.

▶ GETTING STARTED

Think about the question below and then write a short response. There is no right or wrong answer here, so feel free to write the first thing that comes to mind.

In your opinion, what is the best way for each individual person to help protect the environment?

_____

_____

READING

1 The wide variety of natural hazards that can strike at any given time, and the disasters that follow in their wake, serves as a reminder of just how much we depend on our planet's habitable living conditions. Tornadoes, earthquakes, volcanic eruptions, tropical cyclones like hurricanes and typhoons, tidal waves, floods, and
5 various other natural hazards, all have the potential to wreak havoc and lead to the tragic loss of life, with death tolls in some cases measured in the thousands. One type of hazard, though, has seemingly occurred with increasing frequency and intensity in recent years: wildfires. A wildfire is a type of fire that burns out of control on undeveloped land, such as woodlands and prairies, though it can spread so much
10 that it grows to encompass developed land as well. In many cases, such fires are the result of human activities, either negligent or intentional, but they can also be the result of natural causes like lightning. A closer look at a few **specific**[1] cases from different
15 parts of the world can help us better understand this hazard, and how this worldwide problem has the potential to wreak havoc and ruin lives wherever it strikes.

One of Australia's most beloved animal species, the koala has in recent years unfortunately fallen victim to devastating wildfires.

33 **2** Many examples of devastating wildfires can
20 be found in recent history. For instance, Australia has dealt with numerous destructive wildfires, such as the Black Saturday bushfires in February of 2009. Following a heat wave in the southeastern part of the country, powerful winds in excess of a hundred
25 kilometers per hour brought down powerlines, and the resulting sparks triggered a fire that spread rapidly. By the next day, over four hundred separate fires were raging throughout the state of Victoria, with some fires featuring flames that reached thirty meters in height. The fires raged for weeks before firefighters, aided by improving weather conditions, were able to extinguish them.
30 These fires caused **tremendous**[2] damage, and tragically left 173 people dead, 414 people injured, and cost the lives of thousands of livestock animals and countless wild animals. Another example of devastating wildfires can be found in the Mediterranean region. In Greece, for instance, a wildfire near Athens in 2018 was responsible for over a hundred fatalities, and then in 2021, firefighters at one point had to deal with

approximately a hundred active fires on a daily basis. The situation in 2021 grew so terrible that Greece's prime minister reportedly declared that these wildfires were the country's "greatest ecological catastrophe of the last few decades."

34 CD

3 While the danger that wildfires pose to anything standing in their way is obvious, one incident in particular reveals how dangerous they can be to even the 5 very best firefighters who stand on the front lines in an effort to contain such blazes. On June 28, 2013, following a period of excessive heat and an extreme drought in the state of Arizona, in the United States, a lightning strike sparked what came to be known as the Yarnell Hill Wildfire. The fire spread significantly over the next two days, fueled by dry wind, intense heat that reached a hundred degrees Fahrenheit, 10 and intensely dry air of just ten percent relative humidity. On June 30, a specially trained force of firefighters, the Granite Mountain Hotshots, attempted to contain this wildfire near the town of Yarnell. Disaster struck, however, when a sudden and powerful change in the direction of the wind rapidly altered the trajectory and velocity of the fire. The nineteen hotshots were cut off from their escape route, and 15 they tragically all died when the raging flames overtook them. The fire was finally contained on July 10, but this tragedy ended up making the Yarnell wildfire the deadliest in the United States in eighty years, and the day that the hotshots perished was the deadliest day for firefighters in the United States since the 9/11 terrorist attacks. Joe Biden, at the time vice president of the United States, gave a somber 20 eulogy at a memorial service for the fallen hotshots, saying: "… since they chose to be firefighters, since they joined the hotshot crew, you knew they were risking their lives every single time they answered a call."

35 CD

4 Many causes can trigger the start of wildfires: actions by individuals, such as arsonists who deliberately start fires or negligent nature enthusiasts who are careless 25 with their campfires; industrial processes like construction projects and railroads that are in close proximity to forests; and natural events, which are most commonly in the form of lightning strikes. In the United States, for instance, human activities are responsible for nearly eighty-five percent of all wildfires, according to the National Park Service. Though specific incidents related to human activity may be responsible 30 for triggering most wildfires, it appears that changes in environmental conditions are making it easier than ever for wildfires to spread out of control. The National Interagency Fire Center has kept records of wildfires in the United States since 1983, for instance, and the ten years with the largest amount of land destroyed by wildfires have all been since 2004, and the three worst years for destruction were 2015, 2020, 35 and 2017.

5 Ultimately, the threat of wildfires should serve as a warning sign for the health of our planet. Whereas the harsh conditions found on the other seven celestial bodies officially classified as planets in our solar system make it impossible for life to survive, Earth's relatively gentle environmental conditions make it uniquely capable

5　of supporting life. The big concern, however, is that climate change, and anthropogenic climate change in particular, may cause irreparable damage to Earth's ideal environmental conditions. One specific threat that may arise from climate change is an increase in the frequency of intensely hot

太陽系の他の惑星について、章末の Point of Interest を読んでみよう。

10　and dry spells, thereby creating ideal conditions for future wildfires. Given how devastating wildfires can be to people, animals, and property, dealing with the issues that **facilitate**[3] the spread of wildfires is clearly becoming more important than ever.

NOTES

in their wake「その後に」　**tidal wave**「津波」　**wreak havoc**「大被害をもたらす」　**wildfire**「山火事、森林火災」　**encompass**「に及ぶ」　**negligent**「怠った」　**lightning**「落雷」　**devastating**「壊滅的な」**bushfire**「森林火災」　**powerline**「送電線」　**trigger**「引き金となる」　**Victoria**「ビクトリア（オーストラリア南東部の州）」　**firefighter**「消防士」　**extinguish**「消す」　**livestock**「家畜類」　**fatality**「死亡者数」　**ecological**「生態上の」　**catastrophe**「大惨事」　**drought**「干ばつ」　**Granite Mountain Hotshots**「グラナイト・マウンテン・ホットショッツ（消防隊）」　**contain**「食い止める」　**trajectory**「進路、経路」　**velocity**「速度」　**hotshot**「消防士」　**deadly**「致命的な」　**Joe Biden**「ジョー・バイデン(1942−) 2009−2017年米国副大統領、2021年より米国第46代大統領」　**somber**「重苦しい」　**eulogy**「弔辞」　**arsonist**「放火犯」　**in close proximity**「すぐ近くに」　**National Park Service**「国立公園局」**National Interagency Fire Center**「全米省庁合同火災センター」　**anthropogenic**「人間の活動に起因する」　**irreparable**「回復できない」

▌VOCABULARY

For each underlined word below, choose the option that most closely approximates its meaning based on the way that it is used in the reading section.

1. … at a few <u>specific</u> cases from different …
   a. detailed　　　**b.** certain　　　**c.** unique

2. … fires caused <u>tremendous</u> damage …
   a. marvelous　　　**b.** formidable　　　**c.** significant

3. … issues that <u>facilitate</u> the spread of …
   a. enable　　　**b.** manage　　　**c.** create

COMPREHENSION QUESTIONS

Read each statement below carefully, and then based on the information presented in this chapter, write "T" if it is true or "F" if it is false.

1. _____ Wildfires burn out of control and are restricted to undeveloped land, such as woodlands and prairies.

2. _____ During the Black Saturday bushfires in 2009, firefighters had to deal with approximately a hundred active fires on a daily basis.

3. _____ Nineteen members of the Granite Mountain Hotshots died in 2013 when raging flames overtook them.

4. _____ The National Interagency Fire Center has kept records of wildfires since 2004, and the three worst years were 2015, 2020, and 2017.

5. _____ A big concern is that climate change may cause irreparable damage to the environment and increase the frequency of hot and dry spells.

PUTTING IT ALL TOGETHER

For each paragraph in the reading section, compose one complete sentence that summarizes the main theme of that paragraph.

Paragraph 1: _____

_____

Paragraph 2: _____

_____

Paragraph 3: _____

_____

Paragraph 4: _____

_____

Paragraph 5: _____

_____

Write a complete sentence that states whether your answer to the question below is "yes" or "no." Then write a sentence that provides support for your answer.

> Are wildfires in a certain country primarily a problem only for those who in live in that country?

_____

_____

_____

_____

① 37 CD

POINT OF INTEREST

Listen carefully to the audio recording for this section and fill in the blanks in the paragraph below.

Earth's closest planetary neighbor, Venus, features 1.) _____ inhospitable conditions, most notably on account of its searing surface temperatures, which reach 470 degrees Celsius. Furthermore, its atmosphere is so 2.) _____ that standing on its surface is the equivalent of being about 1.6 kilometers under water on Earth. Our next nearest neighbor, Mars, features far more 3.) _____ conditions, but they are still far from adequate to support life. The average temperature on the planet's surface is minus 63 degrees Celsius, with lows that reach minus 140 degrees Celsius, and highs that reach a 4.) _____ 30 degrees Celsius. Though such temperatures are conceivably survivable, its atmosphere is a hundred times thinner than Earth's, which means it 5.) _____ the atmospheric conditions needed to sustain life.

RISE OF THE MACHINES

Are human beings becoming obsolete?

技術革新は、人類の歴史において長い間、進歩の原動力としての機能を果たしてきた。しかし、この百年の間にいっそう急速なペースで進んだ科学技術や産業部門における革新は、無数の製造業の仕事を時代遅れのものにした。近年の人工知能の進歩により、今やサービス業さえ取って代わられている。人間は時代遅れになりつつあるのだろうか。

Machines have long displaced human workers in industrial jobs, but advances in artificial intelligence are now leading to the displacement of human workers in additional sectors of the economy.

▌ GETTING STARTED

Think about the question below and then write a short response. There is no right or wrong answer here, so feel free to write the first thing that comes to mind.

In your opinion, what machine or piece of technology invented in the last hundred years has had the biggest impact on daily life for people?

_____

_____

READING

1 Machines becoming sentient and then lashing out at humans is a popular theme in science fiction films and novels. The book and film *2001: A Space Odyssey*, the *Terminator* film series, and the *Matrix* films, for instance, depict a future in which artificial intelligence (AI) gains the capacity for self-awareness, which then
5 leads to some form of fight for survival between humans and machines. This man-versus-machine sub-genre in science fiction is partly rooted in the tension between the benefits that mechanization offers humanity and the threats that come with such advancements. Though technological **innovation**[1] has long served as the engine of progress throughout human history, the dawn of the twentieth century saw the
10 commencement of what seems like a relentlessly accelerating pace of innovation in the technology and industrial sectors. Technology over the past century has evolved at such an unprecedented pace that, as we will see in this chapter, it is worth pondering the possibility that human beings may one day become obsolete.

2 Much of what we enjoy today, in terms of material comforts, would be
15 impossible without machines in the workforce. Automation and, increasingly, AI are taking over tasks previously handled by human beings. In the simplest terms, technological progress is the product of people building rudimentary machines, and then these machines in turn making it possible to build increasingly powerful and complex machines. With each new
20 wave of machines, however, previously useful human skillsets become obsolete, and the need for new skillsets arise to work with and **supplement**[2] the new wave of machines. According to a 2020
25 World Economic Forum study, which looked at fifteen industries in twenty-six countries, the shift toward greater use of machines and AI could lead to a

Automated assembly lines have made numerous manual labor jobs obsolete.

loss of approximately eighty-five million jobs by 2025, though this shift could also
30 lead to the creation of ninety-seven million new jobs. As the World Bank's *World Development Report 2019* highlights, however, predictions about job losses due to automation and new technology can vary considerably, with some studies projecting significant losses and others projecting comparatively fewer job losses.

3 Throughout much of the twentieth century, job losses due to technological innovation were in the industrial sector, where automation displaced many manual laborers. In recent decades, however, jobs in the service sector are increasingly being lost to AI. Advanced driver-assistance systems in cars, computer-generated opponents in digital games, voice-enabled interactive search engines, auto-complete programs in word processors and phones, for instance, all employ some degree of 5 AI. This kind of programming has made it possible to replace human workers with AI in customer service jobs, for example. It appears that as AI programs feature increasingly sophisticated algorithms with each passing generation, more and more jobs will likely be lost to automated programs.

41 🖥️CD

4 Just how advanced might AI become? A company named DeepMind, part of 10 Google's parent company Alphabet Inc., created an advanced software program called AlphaGo. This program taught itself to play the game of go by watching thousands of human matches. It then went on to defeat several top human go players from 2015 to 2017. AlphaGo Zero, its successor, taught itself to play by playing matches against itself, and after merely forty days it surpassed every version of 15 its predecessor. As powerful as such programs are, however, there is no **indication**[3] that any AI program will become self-aware any time soon. In other words, computer programs are nowhere near achieving self-awareness or expressing a will

人間対コンピュータの
試合について、章末の
Point of Interest を読んで
みよう。

of their own. This means that even though complex algorithms can fulfill many 20 functions that have traditionally relied on human thinking abilities, there are no programs on the horizon that will be able to take on tasks that require original thought, emotional depth, or a will to succeed.

42 🖥️CD

5 Ultimately, the role of machines in society will likely continue to grow indefinitely. Mechanization and automation have steadily replaced manual labor, 25 and more recently, AI has increasingly taken over jobs in the service sector. While different studies disagree about whether technological innovation leads to a net gain in jobs or a net loss in jobs, all studies concur that technological innovation leads to changes in demand for specific types of skills. Such changes unfortunately tend to have a disparate impact socially and globally, and so the world's most economically 30 vulnerable tend to bear the brunt of this impact when certain sectors of the economy incorporate new technological innovations. This means that even though there is no indication that machines are on the verge of becoming self-aware and then launching a war against humanity as depicted in many sci-fi stories, it is clear that they unfortunately represent a very real threat economically to certain segments of 35 society whose livelihoods are based on jobs that technological innovation can one day make obsolete. It is therefore important to not only invest in social safety nets that focus on educational opportunities and training programs for those whose jobs are displaced by technological innovations, but to also consider ways to offer direct assistance in situations where more jobs are lost than created by new technologies.

NOTES

sentient「知覚のある」 **lash out at**「突然食ってかかる」 **depict**「描写する」 ***2001: A Space Odyssey*** 「『2001年宇宙の旅』」 ***Terminator***「『ターミネーター』」 ***Matrix***「『マトリックス』」 **self-awareness**「自己認識」 **obsolete**「時代遅れの」 **rudimentary**「初期段階の」 **skillset**「人間の技能範囲」 **World Economic Forum** 「世界経済フォーラム（各国の企業や団体が加盟する非営利団体）」 **AlphaGo**「アルファ碁、アルファご」 **AlphaGo Zero**「アルファゴ・ゼロ」 **surpass**「勝る」 **concur**「同意する」 **disparate**「共通点がない」 **vulnerable**「弱い」 **bear the brunt**「矢面に立つ」 **incorporate**「取り入れる」 **on the verge of**「の寸前である」 **livelihood**「生計」

VOCABULARY

For each underlined word below, choose the option that most closely approximates its meaning based on the way that it is used in the reading section.

1. … technological <u>innovation</u> has long served …

    a. change   **b.** influence   **c.** invention

2. … arise to work with and <u>supplement</u> the new …

    a. complement   **b.** replace   **c.** transform

3. … there is no <u>indication</u> that any AI program …

    a. warning   **b.** sign   **c.** truth

COMPREHENSION QUESTIONS

Read each statement below carefully, and then based on the information presented in this chapter, write "T" if it is true or "F" if it is false.

1. _____ Science fiction's man-versus-machine sub-genre is partly rooted in the fear of technological advancements.

2. _____ A World Economic Forum study shows that new technology in the workplace could lead to an overall gain of twelve million jobs.

3. _____ Throughout much of the twentieth century job losses were due to the growth of artificial intelligence.

4. _____ AlphaGo Zero within a mere forty days of teaching itself to play go became superior to every version of AlphaGo.

5. _____ Virtually all studies agree that introducing new technology in the workplace leads to a net loss of jobs.

PUTTING IT ALL TOGETHER

For each paragraph in the reading section, compose one complete sentence that summarizes the main theme of that paragraph.

Paragraph 1: _____

_____

Paragraph 2: _____

_____

Paragraph 3: _____

_____

Paragraph 4: _____

_____

Paragraph 5: _____

_____

Write a complete sentence that states whether your answer to the question below is "yes" or "no." Then write a sentence that provides support for your answer.

> Even though there is no indication that artificial intelligence is on the cusp of achieving self-awareness, can it still pose a threat to people?

_____

_____

_____

_____

① 43 CD

POINT OF INTEREST

Listen carefully to the audio recording for this section and fill in the blanks in the paragraph below.

A chess match in 1996 between world chess champion Garry Kasparov and an IBM supercomputer named Deep Blue 1.) _____ a turning point in the development of artificial intelligence. Deep Blue stunned the world by winning the first game 2.) _____ the human world chess champion, though Kasparov went on to win the match with three wins and two ties in the following five games. The supercomputer displayed impressive skills, but it lost because despite its computational prowess, it could not 3.) _____ its strategy to counteract the adjustments that Kasparov made after he lost the first game. Deep Blue 4.) _____ improvements and modifications the following year, and this time won twice, tied three times, lost once, and thus stunned Kasparov by winning the match. Although Deep Blue's computational power seems impressive since it could consider up to two-hundred million moves per second, it is perhaps not that impressive when considering that there are more 5.) _____ ways for a game of chess to play out than there are atoms in the observable universe.

THE CALL OF THE WILD

Chapter 8

Why do humans and dogs have such a special bond?

様々な動物種がコンパニオン・アニマルとしての役割を果たしているが、犬が特別な位置を占めているのは紛れもない事実だ。人間の家族と一緒に暮らす犬との感情面での絆を見ても、あるいは警察などで働く犬との実践的な面での絆を見ても、人間と犬の結びつきはとても強い。人間と犬はどのような経緯でこのような関係を築くことになったのか。また、なぜ犬は私たちの社会で特別な存在なのだろうか。

Jack London's *The Call of the Wild* is an adventure novel about a dog whose journey back into the wild allows him to rediscover his primitive wolf-like instincts. In the real world, however, many dog breeds, like the French Bulldog breed pictured above, depend so heavily on humans for survival that it would be all but impossible for them to survive in the wild.

◀ GETTING STARTED

Think about the question below and then write a short response. There is no right or wrong answer here, so feel free to write the first thing that comes to mind.

How much interaction have you personally had with companion animals, like dogs, throughout your life?

_____

_____

READING

1 When it comes to choosing a companion animal, as with many things in life, it is generally a matter of personal preference. Several animal species commonly serve as companion animals, such as cats, certain types of fish, certain bird species, various small rodents and reptiles, and certain working animals like horses. For many

5   people, however, there is no animal species that holds a more **privileged**[1] place in a human family than *Canis familiaris*—the domestic dog. The relationship between humans and dogs has a lengthy history, and in fact, dogs are the only animals that were domesticated before humans developed agriculture and established permanent settlements. How exactly dogs came to be so closely connected to humans, however,

10 remains a mystery. Let us therefore take a closer look at the history of the relationship between dogs and humans in order to better understand how that relationship evolved over time to make dogs, as the expression goes, "man's best friend."

2 Precisely when and where humans first domesticated dogs remains unclear. According to one study based on recent DNA analysis of thirty-five-thousand-year-old

15 wolf remains from northern Russia, dogs appear to have split from a now-extinct wolf species sometime between twenty-seven thousand to forty thousand years ago. As for when humans domesticated dogs, there is archeological evidence that suggests that

20 this development likely occurred at least twenty thousand years ago. Humans in hunter-gatherer groups likely first domesticated dogs to help them with hunting, or for companionship, or for both purposes. The discovery of human and dog remains

25 in the early twentieth century in Bonn-Oberkassel, Germany, represents the oldest confirmed case of humans keeping domesticated dogs for companionship. The remains feature two humans and two dogs who were apparently buried together

30 approximately fourteen thousand years ago. This

Dating back at least 2,200 years in China, the Chow Chow is one of the oldest dog breeds.

means that even though there is currently no way to know when and why humans domesticated dogs in the first place, humans treating dogs as pets in much the same way that people today see dogs as part of their family is a phenomenon that is likely at least fourteen thousand years old.

03 CD

3 Although dogs today most commonly serve as companion animals first and foremost, over the course of thousands of years humans have been selectively breeding them to **fulfill**[2)] specific functions. Some dogs were bred, for instance, to develop an unparalleled sense of smell that is useful for tracking, with three of the most notable breeds being the Bloodhound, the Basset Hound, and the Grand 5 Bleu de Gascogne, all originally bred in France. Other dogs were bred to develop strong herding and guarding skills, with three of the most notable breeds being the German Shepherd Dog, the Dobermann, and the Rottweiler, all originally bred in Germany. In other cases, dogs were bred to be durable 10 and skilled in hunting, such as the Hokkaido, the Akita, and the Shiba Inu, all originally bred in Japan. Though all of these various breeds are now commonly kept as companion animals, their skills in some cases have found professional use in the modern world, such as the Bloodhound as a tracking dog, or the German Shepherd as a police dog. 15

> キツネが人間に繁殖され飼いならされた過程について、章末の Point of Interest を読んでみよう。

04 CD

4 Many dog species, however, are purely companion animals. Chihuahuas, Miniature Poodles, and Jack Russell Terriers, just to name a few, lack the size and instincts that would make them useful to assist humans in activities like detecting dangerous substances or chasing criminal suspects, but they are as capable as any other breed for serving as companion animals. One of the best examples of 20 dogs being bred purely for the purposes of companionship is the French Bulldog. This breed is the result of mixing two types of dogs that did indeed serve specific functions: small French rat-catching dogs and English Bulldogs, whose bulky frames and large heads made them perfect for bull-baiting matches. The French Bulldog can serve as a great companion animal for humans, but it cannot assist humans with 25 any practical tasks. In fact, these dogs require assistance from humans for some of their most basic needs. For instance, the French Bulldog's head is so large that many females cannot give birth naturally and instead need a surgical procedure to deliver their pups. Moreover, the French Bulldog is a brachycephalic breed, which means that it has a very short snout, and so it runs the risk of experiencing life-threatening 30 respiratory distress when exposed to warm temperatures. French Bulldog owners, however, clearly find that this breed's charming appearance and unique personality make it so appealing that they are perfectly content to take on extra responsibilities in exchange for absolutely nothing other than companionship.

05 CD

5 In the end, then, it is clear that dogs and humans in general have forged 35 a **profound**[3)] bond and, in some cases, a productive working relationship over the

thousands of years since dogs were domesticated. Humans today throughout various parts of the world value dogs primarily as companion animals, so much so that many households view dogs as members of the family. Many dog breeds also serve practical roles in society, such as the German Shepherd in police work and the
5　Golden Retriever as an assistant dog for people with physical disabilities. As close as the human-dog bond is, however, countless dogs end up in animal shelters, where they are confined in small cages and then often euthanized. Such dogs are usually either strays who never had a home in the first place, or they are cast aside by pet owners who can no longer take care of them. This is clearly an unfitting situation for
10　a species that has long offered such loyal companionship, and so it is vital to increase efforts to educate potential pet owners about the challenges that come with pet ownership, to spay and neuter dogs when appropriate in order to prevent the growth of stray populations, and to encourage people to adopt from animal shelters rather than buy puppies from retail outlets.

NOTES

rodent「齧歯（げっし）類」　**reptile**「爬虫類」　**domesticate**「飼いならす」　**remains**「遺体（化石）」　**now-extinct**「今では絶滅した」　**archeological**「考古学の」　**hunter-gatherer**「狩猟採集民」　**herd**「追い立てる」　**bulky**「大きくどっしりした」　**bull-baiting**「ブルベイティング（英国で行われていた雄牛に犬をけしかける見せ物で19世紀に禁止された）」　**surgical procedure**「外科手術」　**pup**「子犬」　**brachycephalic**「短頭の」　**snout**「鼻」　**life-threatening**「命にかかわる」　**respiratory distress**「呼吸困難」　**euthanize**「安楽死させる」　**spay**「不妊手術を施す」　**neuter**「去勢する」

◤ VOCABULARY

For each underlined word below, choose the option that most closely approximates its meaning based on the way that it is used in the reading section.

1. … holds a more <u>privileged</u> place in a …
   a. inexplicable　　　**b.** challenging　　　**c.** special

2. … breeding them to <u>fulfill</u> specific …
   a. finish　　　**b.** satisfy　　　**c.** start

3. … in general have forged a <u>profound</u> bond …
   a. complicated　　　**b.** deep　　　**c.** strange

◀ COMPREHENSION QUESTIONS

Read each statement below carefully, and then based on the information presented in this chapter, write "T" if it is true or "F" if it is false.

1. _____ Of all domesticated animals, dogs are the only ones that were domesticated before humans developed agriculture.

2. _____ The oldest confirmed case of keeping dogs for companionship is from archeological evidence from twenty thousand years ago.

3. _____ The Bloodhound has an unparalleled sense of smell that is useful for tracking, and was originally bred in Germany.

4. _____ The French Bulldog is a brachycephalic breed, which means that its head is so large that many females cannot give birth naturally.

5. _____ The German Shepherd is good for police work and the Golden Retriever is good at assisting people with physical disabilities.

◀ PUTTING IT ALL TOGETHER

For each paragraph in the reading section, compose one complete sentence that summarizes the main theme of that paragraph.

Paragraph 1: _____

_____

Paragraph 2: _____

_____

Paragraph 3: _____

_____

Paragraph 4: _____

_____

Paragraph 5: _____

_____

DEBATING THE ISSUES

Write a complete sentence that states whether your answer to the question below is "yes" or "no." Then write a sentence that provides support for your answer.

> Does the author hold a purely favorable view of the relationship between dogs and humans?

_____

_____

_____

_____

② 06

POINT OF INTEREST

Listen carefully to the audio recording for this section and fill in the blanks in the paragraph below.

Soviet geneticist Dmitri Belyaev undertook a bold scientific experiment in 1952 to domesticate the silver fox, which is closely 1.) _____ to the wolf and the domestic dog. One of his colleagues, Nina Sorokina, was the chief breeder at a farm in a 2.) _____ part of Estonia that housed approximately fifteen hundred foxes. Most of these foxes were fiercely 3.) _____ or terribly frightened of humans, but a few were calm enough to manage reasonably. They selected the calmest ones and bred them, then selected the calmest pups from the 4.) _____ litters and eventually bred them, and so on. In 1959, he partnered with another colleague, Lyudmila Trut, and initiated a large-scale domestication experiment that in the span of just a few decades successfully 5.) _____ foxes that were essentially just as friendly and loyal as dogs.

READY FOR LAUNCH

Chapter

9

How is the private sector transforming space travel?

人類が初めて月面に着陸してから 50 年以上が経つことを考えると、いまだに宇宙旅行が比較的少数の宇宙飛行士のみに限られているのは、ある意味信じがたいことである。民間の宇宙旅行会社がビジネスを始めるようになりつつある今、宇宙旅行はついに一般の人々にも、近いうちに手が届くようになるのだろうか。

Apollo 11 astronaut Neil Armstrong, the first man to set foot on the Moon, stands near the lunar lander Eagle.

GETTING STARTED

Think about the question below and then write a short response. There is no right or wrong answer here, so feel free to write the first thing that comes to mind.

If you were given an opportunity to take a trip to space for free, as a space tourist, would you accept, and why or why not?

_____

_____

READING

07

1 On July 20, 1969, American astronaut Neil Armstrong became the first person to set foot on the Moon. As he took his first step on the lunar surface, he famously declared: "that's one small step for [a] man, one giant leap for mankind." Many watching on television back on Earth likely believed that this first step on the Moon could be the first step to making space travel available for even regular people. However, following the historic Apollo 11 mission's successful Moon landing, the National Aeronautics and Space Administration (NASA) completed only five more manned lunar landings, meaning that a total of only twelve people have walked on the Moon. Moreover, only professional astronauts from national space programs like NASA, with very few exceptions, have been able to venture out into space. As we will see in this chapter, though, recent developments in the private sector may be on the verge of making space travel **accessible**[1] to a much broader segment of the population.

古代神話に登場する人間
の飛行について、章末の
Point of Interest を読んで
みよう。

08

2 The year 1957 marks the dawn of the space age, for it was then that the Soviet Union successfully launched the first man-made object, a satellite named Sputnik, into orbit. It was a stunning victory of sorts over the communist country's geopolitical rival, the United States, given that the two countries devoted **massive**[2] resources to expanding their influence on land, water, and even in space. The Soviet Union scored another major victory in 1961 by launching the first human, Yuri Gagarin, into space. Though the Soviet Union had come to dominate the early phases of the space race, the biggest prize of all remained up for grabs—the Moon. Landing on the Moon first allowed the United States to effectively declare victory in the space race, which led NASA to begin focusing more on sending unmanned research missions to various parts of the Solar System, and sending professional astronauts into orbit around Earth for scientific research.

09

3 NASA launched several notable unmanned missions. In 1976, for instance, Viking 1 became the first spacecraft to land on Mars. The following year, NASA launched a pair of satellites to study the outer Solar System, Voyager 2 and then two weeks later Voyager 1. After the satellites passed by Jupiter and Saturn, Voyager 1 began to head out of the Solar System, while Voyager 2 went on to pass by Uranus and Neptune before proceeding to also head out of the Solar System. Voyager 1 became the first satellite to enter interstellar space in 2012, while Voyager 2 went on to enter interstellar space six years later. As for manned space missions, NASA's Space Shuttle

Program became central to American space travel when it first launched in 1981. The reusable spacecraft transported astronauts into orbit and to the International Space Station (ISS), until the Space Shuttle Program was terminated in 2011.

4 The discontinuation of the Space Shuttle Program has helped dramatically increase the private sector's influence on space travel. One of the most influential 5 private companies is Space Exploration Technologies Corp., simply called SpaceX, founded by Elon Musk. In 2020, SpaceX became the first private company to transport astronauts to the ISS when it launched a spacecraft carrying two NASA astronauts. The company also sent its first four space tourists, who went into orbit on a three-day mission, in September of 2021. In July of 2021, a company named Virgin 10 Galactic, founded by Richard Branson, launched its first passenger space flight, which included Branson himself as a passenger. Also in July of 2021, Blue Origin, LLC, a company founded by Jeff Bezos, launched its first passenger flight, which included Bezos himself as a passenger. Though neither Virgin Galactic nor Blue Origin reached orbit like SpaceX did, the Blue Origin flight crossed the Kármán line. Set by the Fédération Aéronautique Internationale (FAI), the Kármán line delineates the boundary between Earth's 20

NASA's Space Shuttle Columbia takes off in 1981 for a test flight.

atmosphere and outer space at one hundred kilometers above sea level. In October of that same year, Blue Origin followed up with a second space flight, which included as a passenger one of the most inimitable figures in the history of space travel in 25 the world of science fiction: William Shatner, who played James T. Kirk, captain of the iconic starship U.S.S. Enterprise in the *Star Trek* television series and motion pictures. The ninety-year-old Shatner became the oldest person ever to travel into space.

5 What does the future hold, then, for those who hope to travel into space? For 30 one thing, travel to the Moon or another planet, such as Mars, will likely remain out of reach for a long time. In 2017, then President Donald Trump signed Space Policy Directive 1, which calls on NASA to establish a lunar base that will be used as a starting point for a manned mission to Mars. While landing astronauts on the Moon again sometime this decade, or certainly in the 2030s, is a **distinct**[3)] possibility, it 35 appears that tourism opportunities to the lunar surface are at least several decades

away. As for Mars, national space programs and private companies have proposed sending humans to the Red Planet, but it is unlikely that anything like space tourism to our planetary neighbor will be realized any time soon. Secondly, private space flights are rather expensive, currently costing hundreds of thousands of dollars per
5 seat. As such, getting up into space will likely remain out of reach for most people for quite some time, which raises questions about the benefits of having a space tourism industry. If recent developments are going to yield just another luxury for the world's wealthiest, then there is obviously little reason for enthusiasm. On the other hand, if these recent advances genuinely mark the beginning of an industry
10 that, as it grows, will eventually be able to cut costs enough to make space travel reasonably affordable for many, then these are exciting times indeed.

NOTES

astronaut「宇宙航空士」　Neil Armstrong「ニール・アームストロング(1930−2012)」　lunar「月の」　National Aeronautics and Space Administration「米国航空宇宙局」　stunning「衝撃的な」　geopolitical「地政学的」　Yuri Gagarin「ユーリイ・ガガーリン(1934−68)」　up for grabs「誰にでも簡単に手に入る」　Jupiter「木星」　Saturn「土星」　Uranus「天王星」　Neptune「海王星」　interstellar「恒星間の」　reusable「再利用できる」　terminate「打ち切る」　discontinuation「中止、中断」　Elon Musk「イーロン・マスク(1971−) 米国の実業家、エンジニア、投資家」　Richard Branson「リチャード・ブランソン(1950−) イギリスの実業家」　Jeff Bezos「ジェフ・ベゾス(1964−) 米国の実業家、投資家、慈善事業家、Amazon.com の共同創設者」　Kármán line「カーマン・ライン(海抜高度100キロメートルに引かれた仮想のライン)」　Fédération Aéronautique Internationale「国際航空連盟」　delineate「境界を示す」　boundary「境界」　inimitable「独特の」　William Shatner「ウィリアム・シャトナー(1931−) カナダの俳優」　starship「宇宙船」　Donald Trump「ドナルド・トランプ(1946−) 米国第45代大統領」　Space Policy Directive 1「宇宙政策指令第1号」　the Red Planet「赤い惑星（火星の俗称）」　affordable「手頃な」

▶ Vocabulary

For each underlined word below, choose the option that most closely approximates its meaning based on the way that it is used in the reading section.

1. … space travel <u>accessible</u> to a much broader …

   a. potential　　　　**b.** available　　　　**c.** comprehensible

2. … devoted <u>massive</u> resources to expanding …

   a. heavy　　　　**b.** immense　　　　**c.** magnificent

3. … is a <u>distinct</u> possibility …

   a. likely　　　　**b.** rare　　　　**c.** unique

COMPREHENSION QUESTIONS

Read each statement below carefully, and then based on the information presented in this chapter, write "T" if it is true or "F" if it is false.

1. _____ Following the historic Apollo 11 mission's successful Moon landing, only five more people have landed on the Moon.

2. _____ The United States launching Sputnik into orbit was a stunning victory of sorts over the communist country called the Soviet Union.

3. _____ NASA launched a pair of satellites to study the outer Solar System, Voyager 1 and then two weeks later Voyager 2.

4. _____ At ninety years old, William Shatner became the oldest person to travel into space when he flew aboard a Blue Origin spacecraft in 2021.

5. _____ Since Space Policy Directive 1 was signed in 2017, space tourism to Mars should become a reality sometime in the near future.

PUTTING IT ALL TOGETHER

For each paragraph in the reading section, compose one complete sentence that summarizes the main theme of that paragraph.

Paragraph 1: _____

_____

Paragraph 2: _____

_____

Paragraph 3: _____

_____

Paragraph 4: _____

_____

Paragraph 5: _____

_____

DEBATING THE ISSUES

Write a complete sentence that states whether your answer to the question below is "yes" or "no." Then write a sentence that provides support for your answer.

> Does the author argue that recent developments in the private sector indicate that space travel will soon be available for regular people?

_____

_____

_____

_____

② 12 CD

POINT OF INTEREST

Listen carefully to the audio recording for this section and fill in the blanks in the paragraph below.

According to **1.)** _____ Greek mythology, a man named Daedalus was about to incur the wrath of a vengeful king named Minos, and so he created wings out of wax and feathers so that he and his son, Icarus, could escape by air. As they flew away, Daedalus **2.)** _____ his son not to fly too close to the Sun. Icarus got caught up in the excitement of flight, however, and ended up soaring so high that the Sun melted the wax holding his wings together, resulting in a **3.)** _____ plunge into the ocean below. The intended moral of this story centers of the importance of listening to one's elders and avoiding **4.)** _____, but it also long served as a symbolic tale of sorts for humanity's seemingly doomed quest for flight. That all changed dramatically in the span of less than two centuries when air travel went from two French brothers, Joseph-Michel Montgolfier and Jacques-Etienne Montgolfier, **5.)** _____ the first manned flight in a hot air balloon in 1783, to two American astronauts, Neil Armstrong and Edwin "Buzz" Aldrin Jr., landing on the Moon in 1969.

THE MIND'S EYE

Is the world around us what it actually appears to be?

私たちの身の回りの世界は、我々の五感が伝える通りだと単純に考えたくなる。しかし、歴史を通して一部の哲学者たちは、物質界は見かけとは違う可能性を提起してきた。これは確かに、立ち止まって考えてみる価値がある。私たちの周りの世界は、本当は見かけ以上のものが存在しているのだろうか。

As people observe the world around them, it is not unusual for them to question the nature of reality.

▌GETTING STARTED

Think about the question below and then write a short response. There is no right or wrong answer here, so feel free to write the first thing that comes to mind.

Here is a classic thought experiment: if a tree falls in the woods, and no one is there to hear it fall, does it still make a sound?

_____

_____

READING

1 The nature of reality has long been a subject of philosophical inquiry. The simplest way to characterize reality is by defining it as that which exists independently of our perceptions. This simplistic definition suggests that it is the physical world around us that constitutes reality, given that it presumably exists whether or not we
5 perceive it. We derive our knowledge of the physical world from hearing, touching, smelling, tasting, and looking at things. We connect these sensory experiences to a vocabulary that makes it possible for us to think about all of these diverse experiences even when we are not actually experiencing them. People therefore understand what the color blue is, even when not looking at something blue, and people understand
10 what hot water is even when not actually touching hot water. Since everything we know about the world is based on our perceptions, however, an **obvious**[1] problem arises when we try to conceptualize reality: how do we know if these things that we experience actually look, smell, taste,
15 feel, and sound the way that we think they do? As we will see in this chapter, there is more than meets the eye when it comes to declaring that the physical world around us is what constitutes reality.

A shadow outline of a saguaro cactus conceals much of this plant's true features.

2 Several philosophers throughout history
20 have raised the prospect of the physical world not being what it seems. The ancient Greek philosopher Plato, for instance, addresses this question in his penultimate work, *Republic*. In an example that is commonly referred to as the "Allegory of the Cave,"
25 Plato has his readers imagine a bizarre scenario in which a few people have been trapped in a cave since birth. We can simplify this scenario by envisioning that these people are chained up and can only look at a wall that is right in front of them. All they can see, then, are the shadows that real things outside of the cave cast on the wall. For example,
30 when an animal walks by the mouth of the cave during daylight, that animal casts a shadow inside the cave. According to Plato, these people would mistakenly believe that the shadows were actually real animals since they have never seen anything other than shadows. One of the points that Plato seeks to make here is that we may well be like the prisoners in the cave, insofar as we are restricted by what our limited

senses tell us, and so reality is something that lies beyond the reach of our senses.

15

3 Immanuel Kant, an eighteenth-century German philosopher, is one of the most notable philosophers who addresses this issue at length. According to Kant, the physical world around us really does constitute objective reality, which he called *noumena*. Kant postulated the existence of a "thing-in-itself," which is what an object 5 really is, as opposed to what it is as defined by human perception. That is, any given physical object has a true essence, a definite existence, but our human senses cannot fully perceive it. We can never know what it truly is due to the subjective nature of filtering the world through human senses. When someone looks at a tree and listens to its leaves rustling in the wind, for example, that

現実は真に存在するのか という疑念について、章 末 の Point of Interest を 読んでみよう。

10

person's eyes and ears generate sensory **input**[2] based on certain features of the tree's actual physical properties. That person's brain then processes this sensory information into an image that he or she identifies as a tree and a sound that he or she identifies as rustling leaves in the wind.

15

16

4 Our limited senses therefore seemingly lead us to formulate what is merely a subjective evaluation of the physical world. For instance, dogs can hear different frequencies and therefore hear rustling leaves differently, while bees can see ultraviolet and thus see the tree differently. If we consider reality as being the world as it exists independently of our senses, then we can never know what reality truly is since we 20 cannot perceive anything, in Kant's terms, as a thing-in-itself. Hence, we must find ways to mitigate the subjective nature of our senses as we observe the world around us if we want to better understand reality. This is obviously a difficult goal, but this kind of mission statement is not all that different from what scientists have been doing for centuries. The purpose of science, physicist Brian Greene notes, is "to experience 25 the universe on all possible levels," rather than just the levels that happen "to be accessible to our frail human senses." The natural sciences have indeed contributed a great deal to our understanding of reality in the last few centuries, by discovering, for example, sound frequencies and colors that lie beyond human sensory capabilities.

17

5 The bottom line is that it is simply not possible for people to claim that they are 30 experiencing the world around them as it truly is. Aside from sound frequencies and colors that lie beyond human sensory capabilities, there is even more about reality that we may not be able to experience through our senses, and there are aspects of reality that we may not be able to even fully conceptualize. Albert Einstein, for instance, altered our understanding of space-time by introducing the idea of gravitational 35 fields. According to Einstein's work, which was later **confirmed**[3] experimentally, even empty space is something, and this something can bend and twist. Perhaps even more challenging to our understanding of space-time is the work being done in string theory, which is challenging our traditional notion of physical space as being three-dimensional. Superstring theory, for instance, posits that there are nine spatial dimensions, while another version of string theory, called M-theory, posits that there are ten. It is simply impossible for us to visualize these added dimensions, but the theoretical work done by string theorists supports the possibility of their existence. Ultimately, there is clearly much more to the world around us than what we perceive with our senses, and so we obviously cannot claim that the world as we experience it constitutes reality—and though science may give us a better understanding of what the world around us really is, we will likely never be able to truly experience anything in the physical world as, in Kant's terms, a thing-in-itself.

NOTES

sensory「感覚の」　conceptualize「概念化する」　Plato「プラトン (c.427–347b.c.)」　penultimate「最後から2番目の」　*Republic*「『国家』」　allegory「寓話」　bizarre「奇怪な」　envision「心に描く」　chain up「鎖で縛り上げる」　Immanuel Kant「イマヌエル・カント(1724–1804)」　thing-in-itself「物自体」　rustle「サラサラという」　ultraviolet「紫外線」　mitigate「軽減する」　Brian Greene「ブライアン・グリーン(1963–)」　frail「弱い」　the bottom line「要点、肝心なこと」　Albert Einstein「アルベルト・アインシュタイン(1879–1955)」　gravitational field「重力場」　space-time「時空」　string theory「ひも理論」　superstring theory「超ひも理論」　posit「仮定する」　spatial dimension「空間次元」　visualize「視覚化する」

◤ VOCABULARY

For each underlined word below, choose the option that most closely approximates its meaning based on the way that it is used in the reading section.

1. … an <u>obvious</u> problem arises when …
   a. unremarkable　　**b.** evident　　　　**c.** irrelevant

2. … generate sensory <u>input</u> based on certain …
   a. signals　　　　**b.** ideas　　　　　**c.** emotions

3. … which was later <u>confirmed</u> experimentally …
   a. complicated　　**b.** planned　　　　**c.** validated

◀ COMPREHENSION QUESTIONS

Read each statement below carefully, and then based on the information presented in this chapter, write "T" if it is true or "F" if it is false.

1. _____ The easiest way to define reality is to say that the physical world around us constitutes reality.

2. _____ The point of Plato's allegory of the cave is that our senses may not allow us to know what the real world is actually like.

3. _____ The physical world around us, according to Kant, constitutes an objective reality, but our human senses cannot fully perceive it.

4. _____ Science can mitigate the subjective nature of our senses so that we can better understand reality.

5. _____ Albert Einstein's theory posits that there are nine spatial dimensions, while string theory posits that there are ten spatial dimensions.

◀ PUTTING IT ALL TOGETHER

For each paragraph in the reading section, compose one complete sentence that summarizes the main theme of that paragraph.

Paragraph 1: _____

_____

Paragraph 2: _____

_____

Paragraph 3: _____

_____

Paragraph 4: _____

_____

Paragraph 5: _____

_____

DEBATING THE ISSUES

Write a complete sentence that states whether your answer to the question below is "yes" or "no." Then write a sentence that provides support for your answer.

> Is it just a matter of time before new scientific discoveries make it possible for us to see the world around us as it truly is?

_____

_____

_____

_____

② 18 CD

POINT OF INTEREST

Listen carefully to the audio recording for this section and fill in the blanks in the paragraph below.

The seventeenth-century French philosopher René Descartes, often called the father of 1.) _____ philosophy, argued that it was impossible to be absolutely certain that the world around us is what it appears to be. To make his point, he 2.) _____ a hypothetical scenario of a god-like, yet wicked, being tricking him into believing in the existence of an illusory world that does not actually exist. This 3.) _____ an even more disturbing possibility: could such a being also trick Descartes into believing that he exists even though he actually does not? The French philosopher rejected this possibility since, he reasoned, the very act of asking such a question served as 4.) _____ of his mind's existence. The affirmation of his own existence has become one of the most famous quotes in the history of philosophy: *cogito ergo sum*, which is Latin for "I think, 5.) _____ I am."

AHEAD IN THE POLLS

How reliable are public opinion polls?

世論調査は、現代の公共政策や選挙キャンペーンに大きな影響力を持つようになったが、時として誤っていることや、特定の集団の利益になるように操作されることもあるため、いくつかの懸念があるのも事実である。理想的な状況下では、世論調査はどの程度正確なのか。また、世論調査が不正確な結果をもたらす要因は何か。

Donald Trump, at the time president of the United States, and Joe Biden, at the time former vice president, engaged in a heated exchange while debating during the 2020 presidential election campaign.

GETTING STARTED

Think about the question below and then write a short response. There is no right or wrong answer here, so feel free to write the first thing that comes to mind.

How closely do you follow politics in Japan, the United States, and other countries around the world?

_____

_____

READING

19

1 News programs regularly feature public opinion polls about various social issues. Such polls can prove helpful for policymakers when deciding a course of action by letting them know how the general public views various options for any particular issue. During election campaigns new polls about each candidate's level of support
5　come out weekly in some countries. Polling is especially helpful for politicians during election campaigns since it allows them to see how well they are doing in comparison with other politicians, thereby allowing them to adjust their campaign platform accordingly. Public opinion polling can, however, prove problematic in several ways. For one thing, and most obviously, they can occasionally end up being erroneous. In
10　addition, as with any statistical study, they can be manipulated in ways that serve a particular group's interests. Let us therefore take a closer look at polling to see how accurate it can be under ideal circumstances, and what factors can lead to inaccurate results.

20

2 Public opinion polling has been around for a long time. Back in the nineteenth
15　century, it was relatively commonplace for American newspapers to poll their readers about various political issues, or about which politicians they preferred in upcoming elections. Even though hundreds of thousands of people sometimes responded to poll questions, such polls were not necessarily accurate, since the readers who constituted a particular poll's pool of respondents often did not reflect the overall population.
20　In 1935, however, public opinion polling underwent a radical transformation when an American journalist named George Gallup introduced a new, scientific, approach to polling that made it possible to gauge public opinion quite accurately. Gallup relied on random samples of respondents, and used surveys and statistics to **analyze**[1] the respondents themselves and their responses. This approach gave a more accurate
25　representation of society's political preferences, and ultimately Gallup displayed impressive accuracy in predicting election results.

21

3 Since Gallup first introduced his polling method nearly a century ago, various news organizations, universities, and think tanks now conduct public opinion polling. Methodologies vary, but many organizations that conduct scientific polls generally
30　rely on surveying approximately one thousand respondents, and such polls usually have a margin of error that ranges from approximately three to five percent. Though scientific public opinion polling has an impressive track record when it comes to elections, there have been a few instances when polls were proven wrong. One of the most famous instances involves the 1948 United States presidential election, between

Democratic nominee Harry Truman, Republican nominee Thomas Dewey, and third party candidate Strom Thurmond. Most analysts, along with various polls, including Gallup's poll, predicted that Dewey would win the 1948 election handily. In the case of *the Chicago Daily Tribune*, one of the country's major newspapers at the time, editors were so confident that Dewey would **prevail**[2] that they proceeded to start printing papers on election night with the headline "Dewey Defeats Truman" on the front page before all of the votes had been counted. Shortly after some copies went to press and were sent out for the next morning's

U.S. President Harry Truman holds up a newspaper that incorrectly declared Thomas Dewey the winner of 1948 presidential election.

deliveries, it became clear that Truman had actually prevailed. Truman was later famously photographed holding up a copy of this erroneous paper, apparently jubilant over proving the polls wrong.

22 🔴CD

4 In this case, analysts believe that polls got the election result wrong because much of the polling, including Gallup's, concluded several weeks before the election itself. This is significant because elections are competitive processes, and the dynamics of election campaigns change over time, and in some cases especially as election day nears. In fact, it is not unusual to have a sizeable portion of a country's population undecided right up until just a few days before an election. In other cases, different factors can lead to inaccurate public opinion polls. Recent presidential elections in the United States have yielded unexpected results, most notably in 2016 when Republican nominee Donald Trump defeated Democratic nominee Hillary Clinton, and again in 2020 when Democratic nominee Joe Biden defeated Trump. In the former instance, most polls indicated that Clinton would win, yet Trump prevailed. In the latter instance most polls indicated that Biden would win by a sizeable margin, yet the election ended up being far closer

> 2020年のアメリカ大統
> 領選挙の際の世論調査
> について、章末の Point
> of Interest を読んでみよ
> う。

than most experts had predicted. One reason why polls in these instances ended up being inaccurate may be due to some Trump supporters being unwilling to reveal their true political views to pollsters, since the political **climate**[3] in the United States was so tense during these two elections.

23 🔴CD

5 Ultimately, public opinion polling has become a mainstay in political campaigns and in the news world, and its potentially enormous influence over public policy and electoral outcomes makes erroneous polling a serious concern. In some cases, honest mistakes arise, as when changes in public opinion take place after the results of a poll are published, or when some respondents do not want to reveal their true opinions. In other cases, however, polls can be deliberately misleading.

5   For instance, the way that a poll is conducted, such as the method of selecting the respondents, and the way that questions are phrased, can skew the results in favor of a particular group with certain social and political preferences. This means that people should take the time to look at any given poll's sample size, how respondents were contacted, the margin of error, the specific wording of questions asked, the

10 specific wording for response options provided to respondents, and who conducted the poll. Given how influential polls can be on politicians and voters, it is vitally important for members of the public to scrutinize polling results rather than simply accept them at face value.

NOTES

campaign platform「選挙綱領」 erroneous「誤った」 manipulate「加工する、操作する」 commonplace「ありふれた」 upcoming「間近に迫った」 respondent「回答者」 George Gallup「ジョージ・ギャラップ (1901−84)」 gauge「測る」 methodology「方法」 margin of error「誤差」 track record「実績」 nominee「候補者」 Harry Truman「ハリー・トルーマン(1884−72) 米国第33代大統領」 Thomas Dewey「トマス・デューイ (1902−71)」 Strom Thurmond「ストロム・サーモンド (1902−2003)」 jubilant「喜ぶ」 sizable「相当な」 Hillary Clinton「ヒラリー・クリントン (1947−)」 pollster「世論調査員」 mainstay「頼みの綱」 honest mistake「単純なミス」 skew「ゆがめる」

◤ VOCABULARY

For each underlined word below, choose the option that most closely approximates its meaning based on the way that it is used in the reading section.

1. … statistics to <u>analyze</u> the respondents themselves …

   a. formulate   **b.** discuss   **c.** examine

2. … that Dewey would <u>prevail</u> that they …

   a. win   **b.** dominate   **c.** achieve

3. … since the political <u>climate</u> in the …

   a. situation   **b.** structure   **c.** system

◄ COMPREHENSION QUESTIONS

Read each statement below carefully, and then based on the information presented in this chapter, write "T" if it is true or "F" if it is false.

1. _____ Polling can help politicians during election campaigns by letting them modify their campaign to appeal to more voters.

2. _____ Polls in the nineteenth century were more accurate because they sometimes had responses from hundreds of thousands of people.

3._____ News organizations and universities are improving Gallup's polling method by continually increasing the number of respondents.

4. _____ Most experts and polls prior to the 2020 U.S. presidential election believed that Joe Biden would defeat Donald Trump.

5. _____ The way that questions are phrased can skew a poll's results in ways that benefit certain social and political preferences.

◄ PUTTING IT ALL TOGETHER

For each paragraph in the reading section, compose one complete sentence that summarizes the main theme of that paragraph.

Paragraph 1: _____

_____

Paragraph 2: _____

_____

Paragraph 3: _____

_____

Paragraph 4: _____

_____

Paragraph 5: _____

_____

Write a complete sentence that states whether your answer to the question below is "yes" or "no." Then write a sentence that provides support for your answer.

> Since polls can at times be inaccurate, should we disregard them entirely when we see poll results in news reports?

_____

_____

_____

_____

② 24 CD

POINT OF INTEREST

Listen carefully to the audio recording for this section and fill in the blanks in the paragraph below.

Most public opinion polling in 2020 1.) _____ that Democratic candidate Joe Biden would win the state of Wisconsin by about ten percent more votes than the Republican candidate, and at the time incumbent president, Donald Trump. One poll even 2.) _____ that Biden would win by a massive seventeen percent more votes. However, Biden ended up 3.) _____ winning the state by only one percent more votes than Trump. This could well be one of the best instances of Trump voters perhaps feeling uncomfortable about 4.) _____ their political opinions to pollsters. Moreover, this example ultimately serves as a good reminder that polling can end up being 5.) _____ when dealing with politically tense situations.

BY THE SWORD

How did the Roman Republic turn into an empire?

古代ローマは、ヨーロッパのほぼ全域、北アフリカ、中東を征服した史上最強の帝国として有名であるが、古代ローマが当初、民主的な政治形態を取る小さな都市国家であったことは意外に思われるかもしれない。初期の民主主義は、どのようにして帝国へと変わったのか。そして、この変遷から我々は何を学ぶことができるのだろうか。

While passing by a small village, Julius Caesar allegedly stated: "I would rather be the first man here than the second in Rome." This seems like a fitting quote for a man who went on to seize control of Rome as dictator.

◤ GETTING STARTED

Think about the question below and then write a short response. There is no right or wrong answer here, so feel free to write the first thing that comes to mind.

What is your favorite time period and geographic location in history to research and discuss?

_____

_____

READING

25

1 In 509 BCE, according to the traditional recording of ancient Roman history, the people of Rome overthrew their tyrannical king and founded a republican form of government. This form of government was certainly not democratic in comparison with modern democratic countries, but it featured certain traits that we associate with democratic government, such as regularly scheduled elections, a rudimentary system of checks and balances, and a written set of laws that offered basic protections for Roman citizens. Ancient Rome was initially just a small city-state on the edge of the Tiber River in central Italy, but over the next few centuries, it grew rapidly as it conquered all of Italy, much of Europe, North Africa, and the Middle East. While these conquests enriched Rome and expanded its sphere of influence in the region, the resulting societal transformation precipitated a series of political crises that ultimately made it possible for dictatorship to supplant the city's republican government. It is often said that history offers valuable lessons, so let us therefore take a closer look at the Roman Republic's history to see what led to its downfall, and what lessons its **collapse**¹⁾ can offer the world today.

ローマを建国した伝説の人物について、章末の Point of Interest を読んでみよう。

26

2 Rome's rapid expansion from a small city-state to a large imperial power with territories throughout the Mediterranean world contributed greatly to growing inequality in Roman society. Citizen soldiers had to leave their farms unattended for increasingly lengthy periods while fighting in lands far away from Rome, which gave the city's wealthiest ample opportunity to seize more land and create vast estates, rendering many ordinary citizens landless in the process. This precipitated a series of significant changes in Roman politics, and by the late second century BCE a political division arose between the *populares*, a term that roughly translates as "supporters of the people," and the *optimates*, which roughly translates as "the best men." Rome's complex network of norms, procedures, and written rules had long served as an effective political system that strictly bound political figures to set standards and established limitations as to how they could wield political power. Rome's political system also helped moderate the class conflict between the elite patrician class and the plebeian underclass. This new *populares-optimates* political division, however, escalated centuries-old rivalries between elites and the masses, which tested the limits of Rome's political institutions.

27

3 It was not long before this new political division led to violence. A high-ranking official named Tiberius Sempronius Gracchus feuded with Rome's senators in 133 BCE, and they eventually grew so incensed that they had him beaten to death. A decade later his brother Gaius attained the same high-ranking political office and he, like his brother before him, feuded over similar issues with the Senate. Once again like his brother before him, he too ended up getting beaten to death on orders of the Senate. Three decades later, a complex series of issues and events ultimately led 5 to civil war between Marius, a powerful *populares* politician, and Sulla, a powerful *optimates* political rival. Sulla eventually prevailed and made himself dictator, and then used his power ruthlessly to eliminate political opponents. Sulla retired a few years later in 79 BCE and restored republican government, but his use of military power to achieve his political goals set a dangerous precedent. 10

28 🎧

4 Three of Rome's most powerful men soon after entered into a power-sharing agreement that **effectively**[2] gave them control of the government: Crassus, Pompey, and Julius Caesar. Crassus died in battle fighting abroad in 53 BCE, while Caesar and Pompey in the aftermath became political rivals. Caesar was a successful general who conquered Gaul, 15 what is today France, but when his military command expired in 49 BCE, he feared that his political rivals would have him killed if he returned to Rome without his troops. He therefore marched on the city, fought and won a civil war with Pompey, and made 20 himself dictator. A group of senators sought to restore republican government and thus stabbed him to death on the senate floor in 44 BCE. Instead of restoring Rome's government, however, it merely triggered the start of yet another civil war, this time between 25 Caesar's supporters and his assassins. His supporters, led by his adoptive heir Octavian and Mark Antony, defeated his assassins at the Battle of Philippi in 42

Roman territory stretched out to include much of Europe, including Nyon, Switzerland, where a few traces of Roman structures remain.

BCE. Antony and Octavian eventually ended up going to war with each other as well, with Octavian prevailing in 31 BCE. Octavian then proclaimed himself Rome's 30 de facto emperor—officially marking the end of the Roman Republic, and the start of the Roman Empire.

29 🎧

5 "Those who ignore history," the old adage goes, "are doomed to repeat it." While history may not be truly cyclical as this old proverb suggests, given that the circumstances of every region and era are usually unique and thus often generate 35 novel reasons for specific events, it does not mean that similarities do not exist. Social norms and political institutions may change from one time period to another, but human nature is more consistent, in terms of its capacity for virtues like intellectual curiosity and charity, and its capacity for darker impulses like greed and the desire for power. A better adage, then, is: "history does not repeat, but it rhymes." This seems

5 like an apt saying when comparing Roman and American history, for example, given that both have followed similar patterns, from the way that they threw off the shackles of monarchy to establish a republican form of government, to the way that both rose to superpower status. American history unfortunately seems to rhyme with another development that shaped Rome's history—political violence. With

10 the seemingly **intensifying**[3] partisanship recently seen in U.S. politics, highlighted by heated protests, which has even included protesters unlawfully entering the U.S. Capitol in an effort to delay the certification of the 2020 election results, it is important to remember the Roman experience that once the taken-for-granted legitimacy of official government procedures is violated, it may be impossible to

15 restore.

NOTES

overthrow「廃する」　tyrannical「専制的な」　Tiber River「テヴェレ川」　precipitate「引き起こす」
dictatorship「独裁政治」　supplant「取って代わる」　downfall「転落」　wield「持つ」　patrician class
「貴族階級」　plebeian underclass「平民の下層階級」　Tiberius Sempronius Gracchus「ティベリ
ウス・センプロニウス・グラックス (162–133 b.c.)」　feud「争う」　incensed「激怒した」　Gaius「ガイウス
(Gaius Sempronius Gracchus 153–121 b.c.)」　Marius「マリウス (157–86 b.c.)」　Sulla「スラ (Lucius
Cornelius Sulla 138–78 b.c.)」　ruthlessly「冷酷に」　precedent「先例」　Crassus「クラッスス (Marcus
Licinius Crassus 115–53 b.c.)」　Pompey「ポンペイウス (Gnaeus Pompeius Magnus 106–48 b.c.)」
aftermath「余波」　assassin「暗殺者」　adoptive heir「養子の継承者」　Octavian「オクタビアヌス (Caesar
Augustus 63 b.c.–a.d. 14)、ローマ初代皇帝」　Mark Antony「マルクス・アントニウス (83–30 b.c.)」
Battle of Philippi「フィリッピの戦い」　proclaim「公言する」　de facto「事実上の」　adage「格言」
cyclical「周期的な」　greed「貪欲」　rhyme「呼応する」　apt「ぴったりの、適切な」　shackle「束縛」
the U.S. Capitol「米国連邦議会議事堂」　certification「証明」　legitimacy「合法性、正当性」

VOCABULARY

For each underlined word below, choose the option that most closely approximates its meaning based on the way that it is used in the reading section.

1. … what lessons its collapse can offer …
   a. faint　　　　**b.** failure　　　　**c.** fatigue

2. … that effectively gave them control of …
   a. thankfully　　**b.** essentially　　**c.** terribly

3. … the seemingly intensifying partisanship …
   a. worsening　　**b.** motivating　　**c.** threatening

COMPREHENSION QUESTIONS

Read each statement below carefully, and then based on the information presented in this chapter, write "T" if it is true or "F" if it is false.

1. _____ The Roman Republic was by today's standards comparable to modern democratic countries since it held elections regularly.

2. _____ By the late second century BCE rivalries between elites and the masses began to arise in the Roman Republic.

3. _____ Both Tiberius Gracchus and his brother Gaius ended up being beaten to death as a result of their disputes with Rome's senators.

4. _____ A group of senators managed to restore the Republic's government by stabbing Julius Caesar to death on the senate floor in 44 BCE.

5. _____ Though separated by nearly two thousand years, Roman and American history have followed a few similar patterns.

PUTTING IT ALL TOGETHER

For each paragraph in the reading section, compose one complete sentence that summarizes the main theme of that paragraph.

Paragraph 1: _____

_____

Paragraph 2: _____

_____

Paragraph 3: _____

_____

Paragraph 4: _____

_____

Paragraph 5: _____

_____

DEBATING THE ISSUES

Write a complete sentence that states whether your answer to the question below is "yes" or "no." Then write a sentence that provides support for your answer.

> If history doesn't repeat, as the author points out, does it then mean that there are no lessons to be learned from history?

_____

_____

_____

_____

② 30 CD

POINT OF INTEREST

Listen carefully to the audio recording for this section and fill in the blanks in the paragraph below.

The legend of Rome's origin seems fitting, given the violence that Romans unleashed as they 1.) _____ their reach throughout the Mediterranean, and given the violence that eventually plagued their political system. The legend holds that after a long sequence of events 2.) _____ a mother to abandon her twin newborn boys, a she-wolf discovered the twin brothers and nurtured them until they were adopted by a human couple. The two brothers, named Romulus and Remus, eventually made their way to the banks of the Tiber River to create a new settlement in 753 BCE, which led to a 3.) _____ about who should get to serve as ruler. They decided to wait for a sign from the gods in order to determine who should rule, but violence erupted when Remus 4.) _____ his brother's selfish ruse to make it appear as though the gods had chosen him. Romulus ended up killing Remus during the fighting between the two brothers and their supporters, and so Romulus ended up ruling the city and 5.) _____ it after himself—Rome.

DEMOCRATIC IDEALS

What is democracy?

民主政治は、政治制度のあり方や選挙の実施方法など国によって大きく異なり、また、民主的でないにもかかわらず、民主的であると主張する国もある。このように、「民主主義」という言葉は様々な国で使われている。そもそも「民主主義」とは何なのか。

The ruins of the ancient Acropolis of Athens still stand tall today, with the Parthenon being the most prominent feature of these ruins.

► GETTING STARTED

Think about the question below and then write a short response. There is no right or wrong answer here, so feel free to write the first thing that comes to mind.

When you and your friends have to make a decision as a group, where to go eat out, for example, how do you usually decide?

_____

_____

READING

31

1 Those who live in democratic countries often tout the virtues of democracy and celebrate it as the best form of government. Further reinforcing the perceived virtue of this form of government is the fact that even some clearly despotic countries claim to be democratic, and in some cases even use some form of the word
5 "democracy" in their official state name. Given that democracy has such universal appeal and that so many different countries describe themselves as democratic, it is worth asking: what exactly is democracy? The simplest answer is that a country can rightfully call itself a democracy only if its government protects basic human rights for all who live within its borders, and only if those who run the government have
10 attained their political authority legitimately with consent from the public. When it comes to specifics, however, many variations exist in terms of electoral systems, legal standards, and systems of government. Let us therefore take a closer look at the history of democracy and some of the key institutional variations found in democratic countries around the world.

32

15 **2** The word "democracy" comes from two ancient Greek words that together translate as "rule by the common people," which in practical terms means majority rule. The earliest democracy in recorded history first arose in the ancient Greek city-state of Athens, in the sixth century BCE. It was at this time that an Athenian politician named Solon repealed many of the city's **harsh**[1] laws and initiated a series of reforms
20 that gave citizens the right to participate in government. Though electing people to specific offices to manage the government does not seem particularly unique today, it was revolutionary back then. The city's legal and political framework continued to change over the following decades, during which time Athens developed a system of direct democracy. What made the city's government a direct form of democracy
25 is that important decisions were put to a vote in the city's large assembly, called the *ecclesia*, which was open to all citizens.

33

3 Today, most democratic countries feature a type of government that is a form of indirect democracy, which is usually referred to as representative democracy. Citizens vote for representatives who serve in government and who make all decisions,
30 with only a few rare exceptions, such as national referendums. While ancient Athens may at first glance appear to have offered citizens greater political participation than what countries today offer their citizens, it was hardly a model form of democratic government by today's standards. Citizenship was heavily restricted, since only men whose parents were Athenian could be citizens, and what we today call civil

liberties were not necessarily protected. Democratic countries today, by contrast, not only feature decision-making that is based on majority rule, insofar as citizens can regularly vote for government officials, but they also feature constitutional safeguards that prevent the majority from violating the basic rights of those in the minority—such as freedom of expression, due process, and the right to vote. For this reason, 5 democratic countries like Japan, the United States, and many in Europe are called liberal representative democracies.

34 **CD**

4 Democracy comes in many variations today. First, there are different types of democratic government, which broadly speaking either takes the form of a parliamentary model or the form of a presidential model. Many crucial differences 10 exist between these two forms of government, but the most notable is the way that the country's **chief**[2] decision-maker comes to power. In a parliamentary model, citizens vote for representatives who will serve as members of parliament, and these members 15 essentially determine who will serve as the country's chief decision-maker, who is usually referred to as the prime minister. In a presidential model, by contrast, citizens for all intents and purposes usually vote directly for the president, who serves as the country's 20 chief decision-maker. Second, electoral procedures differ from country to country, but they largely take the form of single-member plurality electoral systems or some form of proportional representation. In the

former instance, whoever gets the most votes wins a particular seat in government, which can lead to situations where one party ends up winning a greater share of the seats than their share of the popular vote.

The first parliament in history was developed in England. Since the Palace of Westminster is where 25 Britain's Parliament congregates, the parliamentary model is also called the Westminster model.

In the latter instance, mechanisms are implemented to ensure that the overall number of officeholders from each party reflects each party's percentage of the popular vote. 30

35 **CD**

5 While discussions about democracy often focus on specific institutional traits and the benefits it offers, no discussion would be complete without taking a moment to also consider the responsibilities that come with citizenship in a democratic country. The writings of two of the nineteenth century's most astute political philosophers can help elucidate this point. Alexis de Tocqueville was a French 35 thinker who made a journey to the United States in the early nineteenth century to study the country's burgeoning democracy. Among his many observations, he found that political participation served as a form of political education that made the country's citizens **fit**[3] for self-governance. One of Tocqueville's contemporaries, a British thinker named John Stuart Mill, later made a similar

5　argument by noting that taking part in politics helps fuel a sense of responsibility, and citizens consequently learn how to evaluate officeholders and policy decisions. Ultimately, then, no matter the variations that distinguish some democratic

民主政治のさらなる詳細について、章末の Point of Interest を読んでみよう。

countries from others, they all have one thing in common: while they generally do
10　a better job of protecting the rights of their citizens than non-democratic forms of government do, they rely on citizens keeping up with politics in order to make sure that democratic governance is the best that it can be.

NOTES

tout「ほめそやす」　**despotic**「専制的な、独裁的な」　**rightfully**「合法的に、正当に」　**legitimately**「合法的に」　**specifics**「細目、詳細」　**majority rule**「多数決原理」　**Athenian**「アテネ人の」　**Solon**「ソロン (c.630–c.560b.c.)」　**repeal**「廃止する」　*ecclesia*「エクレシア、教会堂」　**safeguard**「保証条項」　**due process**「法の適正な手続き」　**for all intents and purposes**「事実上は」　**single-member plurality electoral system**「小選挙区制」　**proportional representation**「比例代表制」　**popular vote**「一般投票」　**officeholder**「議席所有者」　**astute**「明敏な、鋭い」　**elucidate**「解明する」　**Alexis de Tocqueville**「アレクシ・ド・トクヴィル (1805–59)」　**burgeon**「急成長する」　**self-governance**「自治」　**governance**「統治」

◤ VOCABULARY

For each underlined word below, choose the option that most closely approximates its meaning based on the way that it is used in the reading section.

1. … repealed many of the city's <u>harsh</u> laws …

   a. notable　　　　**b.** unusual　　　　**c.** severe

2. … that the country's <u>chief</u> decision-maker …

   a. primary　　　　**b.** toughest　　　　**c.** finest

3. … made the country's citizens <u>fit</u> for …

   a. healthy　　　　**b.** suited　　　　**c.** strong

◤ COMPREHENSION QUESTIONS

Read each statement below carefully, and then based on the information presented in this chapter, write "T" if it is true or "F" if it is false.

1. _____ Some countries are not actually democratic even though they use some form of the word "democracy" in their official name.

2. _____ What made Athens a direct democracy is that all decisions were put to a vote in the city's large assembly, called the *ecclesia*.

3. _____ Democratic countries today are based on majority rule, but also have constitutional safeguards to protect those in the minority.

4. _____ The two main types of democratic government are parliamentary models and presidential models.

5. _____ John Stuart Mill took a trip to the United States to study its government and to learn what can make democracy successful.

◤ PUTTING IT ALL TOGETHER

For each paragraph in the reading section, compose one complete sentence that summarizes the main theme of that paragraph.

Paragraph 1: _____

_____

Paragraph 2: _____

_____

Paragraph 3: _____

_____

Paragraph 4: _____

_____

Paragraph 5: _____

_____

DEBATING THE ISSUES

Write a complete sentence that states whether your answer to the question below is "yes" or "no." Then write a sentence that provides support for your answer.

> Since there are constitutional safeguards in a democratic country, does it matter if citizens keep up with what is happening in politics?

_____

_____

_____

_____

② 36 CD

POINT OF INTEREST

Listen carefully to the audio recording for this section and fill in the blanks in the paragraph below.

Each type of government listed in this chapter has many variations, including different types of parliamentary systems and different types of presidential systems throughout the world, and there are even semi-presidential models that 1.) _____ features from both models. Another notable variation is, of course, what kind of party system is in 2.) _____, whether it is a two-party system or multi-party system. In addition, another 3.) _____ feature of democracy is whether it is a unitary system or a federal system. In a unitary system, as found in France and Japan, the central government 4.) _____ gives, and thus can rescind, certain political and legal decision-making powers to local governments. In a federal system, as found in the United States and Canada, states and provinces have certain legal and decision-making powers separate from the central government, and this separation of powers is constitutionally 5.) _____.

THIS MEANS WAR

What lessons can we learn from ancient conflicts?

残念なことに、戦争は人間社会の黎明期から世界を悩ませてきた。そして今日に至るまで、戦争は常に存在する脅威であり続けている。世界最古の歴史家が、古代ギリシャの2つの強力な都市国家間の有名な戦争について研究し、著書を残している。彼は国家間の戦争の原因を研究した最も早い思想家の一人とみなされている。この古代紛争から現代世界は何を教訓とできるか。

Tensions between the United States of America and the People's Republic of China have increased in recent years, raising concerns of a cold war mentality emerging in the Asia-Pacific region.

▶ GETTING STARTED

Think about the question below and then write a short response. There is no right or wrong answer here, so feel free to write the first thing that comes to mind.

Based on what you read and see in the news, what potential conflict in the world concerns you the most?

_____

_____

READING

37

1 As the label implies, a "realist" view of international relations focuses on the way the world actually is, as opposed to the way the world should be. Though realism, and its many variations, was formally developed in the twentieth century, several of its core principles can be traced back to an ancient Athenian historian
5 named Thucydides, whose sole historical work, commonly titled *The Peloponnesian War*, is about a monumental conflict that took place in ancient Greece. Thucydides actually served as a general in the Athenian military during this epic conflict, but he ended up being exiled from Athens after he was unsuccessful in defending a key city from an enemy invasion. Being exiled from Athens gave him a unique vantage
10 point, for he was able to interview participants and witnesses from both sides. This approach to analyzing the war, whereby he sought to objectively recount events based on Athenian and Spartan perspectives, is the reason why he is widely regarded as the first true historian. Though an account of such an ancient conflict at first glance may seem **irrelevant**[1] today, a closer look reveals that it can still hold some valuable
15 lessons for the modern world.

38

2 Ancient Greece at the time of this conflict was not a single unified country, but was instead made up of independent city-states. These city-states banded together and fought largely in unison when threatened by external powers, most notably when the Persian
20 Empire attacked Greece, first in 490 BCE and then once again in 480 BCE. Following Greek success in fending off both Persian invasions, two city-states, Sparta and Athens, started down a path that would lead to an epic clash between them. While Sparta had
25 long stood as the unrivaled military power in ancient Greece, Athens grew rapidly as a naval power in the aftermath of the Persian invasions. Relations between Sparta and Athens grew increasingly acrimonious, and the two powers ended up fighting a series of
30 armed conflicts from 460 to 446 BCE, after which they agreed to cease hostilities and signed a thirty-year truce. In 431 BCE, however, disputes between their

Thucydides likely died before he could finish writing his history of the war, so his text only covers the war's first twenty-one years.

allies pulled the two major powers into a full-scale war, commonly referred to as the Peloponnesian War, which ended with Sparta defeating Athens in 404 BCE.

39 CD

3 While Thucydides recounts numerous events, two key points in particular stand out as iconic examples of core realist principles. First, his explanation for the start of the Peloponnesian War stands as a classic realist interpretation. He expresses hope that future generations will judge his words useful if they want to gain a clear understanding of past events, but more importantly, however, he adds that 5 "human nature being what it is," learning about this conflict could prove useful to future generations since these events will "at some time or other and in much the same ways, be repeated in the future." This emphasis on the inevitability of war, and the role of human nature therein, lies at the heart of classical realist thought. Furthermore, he outlines several specific grievances and incidents that precipitated 10 the war's outbreak, but he emphasizes that "the real reason for the war" and "what made the war inevitable," as it turns out, "was the growth of Athenian power and the fear which this caused in Sparta." This emphasis on fear and survival, in this case Sparta's desire to wage war on Athens before it could grow too powerful, lies at the heart of realist explanations for war. 15

40 CD

4 The other key point that stands out as a classic principle of realist thinking comes from the account that Thucydides gives of negotiations between Athens and the small island of Melos. Although Melos had remained **nominally**[2] neutral during the war, the Athenians invaded in 416 BCE and gave the island's inhabitants a simple ultimatum: join the Athenian empire or face total destruction. The Melians refused 20 to submit, arguing that it was unjust for the Athenians to subjugate a people who have not taken up arms. The Athenian envoys, according to Thucydides, bluntly argued that the concept of justice applies only to those who are equal in power, and so in practice, "the strong do what they have the power to do and the weak accept what they have to accept." After a lengthy debate, neither side backed down, and so 25 the Athenians proceeded to lay siege to the city. The Melians eventually surrendered unconditionally, at which time Athenian forces executed all of the Melian men, and sold the women and children into slavery. This debate, and its outcome, stands as a classic example of the realist conception of power politics, which is that in essence, power dictates international affairs, not morality. 30

41 CD

5 As it turns out, Thucydides was correct in **anticipating**[3] that conflicts that unfold in the same way as this war did would arise in the future. By way of one example of the similarity between a recent conflict and the Peloponnesian War, Russian President Vladimir Putin ordered an invasion of Ukraine in February of 2022 when his demands were not met, which is reminiscent of the more powerful 35 Athens resorting to force against the weaker Melos when the latter would not accede to the former's demands. Another contemporary parallel is the increasing tension between the United States, the world's established dominant power, and China, the world's most rapidly rising power. Both sides have strong incentives to preserve the status quo, but unresolved territorial issues in the South China Sea and the changing power dynamic between the two countries has fostered an increasingly antagonistic relationship that could lead to a dangerous standoff. Jean-Baptiste Alphonse Karr, a nineteenth-century French author and journalist, once wrote a phrase that is usually translated in English as "the more things change, the more they remain the same." It appears that this may well be a fitting statement for the history of international relations, for certain patterns of behavior that dictated the course of the Peloponnesian War, surely enough, seem to remain a factor in the international arena even today.

戦争が起きるのを防ぐための試みについて、章末の Point of Interest を読んでみよう。

NOTES

Thucydides「ツキディデス (c.460–c.400b.c.)」 *The Peloponnesian War*「『ペロポネソス戦史』」 **epic**「空前の規模の」 **exile**「追放する」 **vantage point**「観点」 **recount**「詳しく述べる」 **in unison**「一致協力して」 **fend off**「撃退する」 **acrimonious**「とげとげしい」 **inevitability**「不可避」 **therein**「そこに」 **wage**「行う」 **Melos**「メロス (イタリア語ミロ、ミロのヴィーナス像が発見された地)」 **ultimatum**「最後通牒」 **Melian**「メロス人」 **subjugate**「征服する」 **bluntly**「単刀直入に」 **back down**「引き下がる」 **lay siege to**「包囲する」 **power politics**「武力外交、権力政治」 **unfold**「展開する」**Vladimir Putin**「ウラジーミル・プーチン(1952–)」 **reminiscent**「思い出させる」 **resort**「頼る、訴える」 **accede**「応じる」 **Jean-Baptiste Alphonse Karr**「ジャンバティスト・アルフォンス・カー(1808–90)」

◤ VOCABULARY

For each underlined word below, choose the option that most closely approximates its meaning based on the way that it is used in the reading section.

1. … an ancient conflict at first glance may seem <u>irrelevant</u> today …
   a. unimportant   **b.** unusual   **c.** extraordinary

2. … Melos had remained <u>nominally</u> neutral …
   a. passionately   **b.** frightfully   **c.** essentially

3. … Thucydides was correct in <u>anticipating</u> that …
   a. rejecting   **b.** foreseeing   **c.** interpreting

COMPREHENSION QUESTIONS

Read each statement below carefully, and then based on the information presented in this chapter, write "T" if it is true or "F" if it is false.

1. _____ Thucydides was exiled from Athens because he failed to defend a key city from an enemy invasion during the war.

2. _____ Acrimonious relations between Sparta and Athens led to the start of the Peloponnesian War in 460 BCE.

3. _____ Thucydides argues that the real reason why war was inevitable was the growing power of Sparta and the fear it caused in Athens.

4. _____ The incident on Melos shows that a weaker power can successfully resist a stronger power.

5. _____ It appears that there are similarities between events in the Peloponnesian War and some current events.

PUTTING IT ALL TOGETHER

For each paragraph in the reading section, compose one complete sentence that summarizes the main theme of that paragraph.

Paragraph 1: _____

_____

Paragraph 2: _____

_____

Paragraph 3: _____

_____

Paragraph 4: _____

_____

Paragraph 5: _____

_____

Write a complete sentence that states whether your answer to the question below is "yes" or "no." Then write a sentence that provides support for your answer.

> Does the author suggest that there are similarities between China-U.S. relations and Sparta-Athens relations?

_____

_____

_____

_____

② 42 CD

POINT OF INTEREST

Listen carefully to the audio recording for this section and fill in the blanks in the paragraph below.

An ancient Latin adage has long dominated military strategy and defense budgets: *si vis pacem, para bellum*—if you want 1.) _____, prepare for war. It seems like a fitting saying in that, until recently, a community that could not 2.) _____ defend itself would be at serious risk of being conquered by a more powerful neighbor. The horrors of the First World War, however, were so 3.) _____ that the global community seemed prepared to finally move past its violent ways. Dubbed "the war to end all wars," a phrase based on an H. G. Wells book about the war, it featured an unprecedented level of death and devastation at the hands of modern mechanized warfare, which thus 4.) _____ many countries to join the League of Nations. This international organization was supposed to 5.) _____ that such horrors would never arise again, but it obviously failed, given that an even more devastating conflict broke out a mere two decades after its creation—the Second World War.

LUCK OF THE DRAW

How important is luck for success in life?

人生に起こることの多くは、運に左右されるように思われる。まれな状況下で不幸な出来事を経験した人はその事態を不運と思い、その逆の経験をした人はその状況を幸運と思うかもしれない。私たちがコントロールできない無数の出来事が、（ほかに適切な言葉がないので）「運」と呼ばれるものによって影響を受けている。「運」とは一体何なのか、そしてそれをコントロールすることはできるのか。

People often associate the concept of luck with gambling, whereby winning or losing is seen as a matter of luck.

◤ GETTING STARTED

Think about the question below and then write a short response. There is no right or wrong answer here, so feel free to write the first thing that comes to mind.

What example first comes to mind of people carrying a special item or performing a specific routine in hopes of getting good luck?

_____

_____

READING

01

1 In an essay titled *The Eighteenth Brumaire of Louis Bonaparte*, Karl Marx states: "Men make their own history, but they do not make it as they please … [they make it] under circumstances existing already, given and transmitted from the past." Though this quote refers to the influence of historical circumstances specifically, it
5 may well apply to a broader discussion about how much control we have over our own fate. In other words, we may be able to control our actions, but our actions are constrained by many things that we cannot control. When and where we are born is one obvious example. By way of another example, countless people, over whom we have no control, do things that affect us every day. The haphazard nature of life in
10 social settings, in short, constantly leads to **incidents**[1] that seem completely random and unexpected, and so it appears as though much of what happens in life comes down to plain old luck. People who end up experiencing unusual circumstances that lead to some unpleasant event may see the situation as unlucky, whereas people who experience the opposite may see the situation as lucky. Given that luck is apparently
15 such an important factor in the outcome of many events in life, it is worth taking a closer look at what exactly people mean when they refer to "luck."

02

2 There are a few different ways to conceptualize luck. In some cases, the terms lucky and unlucky denote what seems like random chance. For instance, a golfer who seemingly hit a perfect shot only to
20 have his or her ball end up striking a bird midflight and then landing in the rough would certainly view this as unlucky. Conversely, it would seem incredibly lucky if a golfer hits a bad shot, but then
25 as the ball landed it got kicked in the right direction by an animal and thereby resulted in a hole-in-one. This conception of luck is quite common in everyday life,

Owing largely to its rarity, the four-leaf clover is the quintessential symbol of good luck.

whereby people call what seems like an unlikely sequence of events, over which they
30 have no control and yet results in a positive or a negative outcome, as either lucky or unlucky.

03

3 In other cases, some people characterize luck in quasi-mystical terms. Some people believe that they are born lucky, while others believe that they are born unlucky. While being born lucky or unlucky could refer to the circumstances into which someone is born, such as having incredibly wealthy parents could be construed as being lucky, it can also refer to a person who seems to experience a higher than average frequency of good luck or bad luck. Those who believe in luck defined in this way may engage in superstitious behavior or carry a certain special item, which varies from culture to culture. Some of the most famous examples of items associated 5 with luck in Western civilization, for example, are four-leaf clovers and, perhaps more bizarrely, a rabbit's foot. Some of the most famous superstitions in Western civilization associated with bad luck include breaking a mirror, which some believe brings seven years of bad luck, and the number thirteen, especially the thirteenth day of the month when it falls on a Friday. 10

04 CD

4 While different people have different perspectives about the concept of luck, scientific perspectives generally reject attributing any sequence of events to luck. What seems like good luck or bad luck in the form of a quasi-mystical force, from a scientific perspective, is likely the result of cognitive biases. A cognitive bias known as confirmation bias, for instance, refers to when people focus on information that 15 supports their preconceptions, while discounting information that conflicts with their preconceptions. As for luck in terms of random chance, it is important to **clarify**[2] that it is technically what *seems* like random chance. No matter how bizarre, fluky, or unexpected a sequence of events may be, the laws of nature dictate that every event has a specific cause. What seems like random chance merely appears that way to us 20 because we cannot possibly know all of the variables that produce certain events. For instance, choosing the winning number on a roulette wheel seems like it is a matter of random chance, but only because we cannot see all of the forces that impel us to choose a particular number, and all of the forces that determine on which number the ball will land. 25

05 CD

5 Ultimately, even if luck in the form of truly random chance or in the form of a quasi-mystical force does not exist, it is clear that countless events beyond our control affect our lives, and for lack of a better term, we may refer to this as luck. Commenting on what we would characterize as luck, the Italian Renaissance writer Niccolò Machiavelli offered some advice, in a book titled *The* 30 *Prince*, that may prove useful. Half of success in life comes down to skill, according to Machiavelli, while half comes down to luck. He further notes that even though one cannot control luck, it is possible to anticipate and prepare for bad luck. One must therefore not only be skilled in terms of having the abilities needed 35 to engage in certain activities, but must also be skilled in anticipating bad luck and

マキャヴェッリがどのように運についての発想を得たのか、章末の Point of Interest を読んでみよう。

having contingency plans in place for when the unexpected happens. Given how much of what happens in life comes down to things beyond a person's control, which we can call luck for simplicity's sake, Machiavelli's **insight**[3] on the matter seems like sage advice.

NOTES

The Eighteenth Brumaire of Louis Bonaparte「『ルイ・ボナパルトのブリュメール18日』(1852) ブリュメール (霧月) はフランス革命暦の第2月の称」　**Karl Marx**「カール・マルクス (1818−83)」　**constrain**「抑制する」 **haphazard**「無計画な」　**incredibly**「非常に」　**quasi-mystical**「半神秘的」　**construe**「解釈する」 **superstitious**「迷信的な」　**bizarrely**「奇妙に」　**cognitive bias**「認知バイアス」　**confirmation bias**「確証 バイアス」　**preconception**「先入観、偏見」　**random chance**「偶然」　**fluky**「まぐれの」　**dictate**「規定する」 **impel**「強いてさせる」　**Niccolò Machiavelli**「ニッコロ・マキャベリ(1469−1527)」　***The Prince***「『君主論』 (1532)」　**contingency**「緊急対策」　**sage**「賢明な」

◤ VOCABULARY

For each underlined word below, choose the option that most closely approximates its meaning based on the way that it is used in the reading section.

1. … leads to <u>incidents</u> that seem completely …

   a. confrontations　　**b.** disasters　　　　**c.** occurrences

2. … it is important to <u>clarify</u> that it is …

   a. explain　　　　　**b.** validate　　　　**c.** quantify

3. … Machiavelli's <u>insight</u> on the matter seems …

   a. concern　　　　　**b.** opinion　　　　**c.** care

COMPREHENSION QUESTIONS

Read each statement below carefully, and then based on the information presented in this chapter, write "T" if it is true or "F" if it is false.

1. _____ The Marx quote applies to discussions about control over one's own fate, but it refers to the influence of historical circumstances.

2. _____ The concept of luck as random chance is based on the idea that sequences of events can result in a positive or negative outcome.

3. _____ Those who believe in luck as a quasi-mystical force believe that they have no control whatsoever over good luck or bad luck.

4. _____ What seems like random chance is actually the result of the laws of nature, and so it is not random at all.

5. _____ Machiavelli argues that luck is responsible for half of success or failure in life, so be prepared to accept failure it if happens.

PUTTING IT ALL TOGETHER

For each paragraph in the reading section, compose one complete sentence that summarizes the main theme of that paragraph.

Paragraph 1: _____

_____

Paragraph 2: _____

_____

Paragraph 3: _____

_____

Paragraph 4: _____

_____

Paragraph 5: _____

_____

Write a complete sentence that states whether your answer to the question below is "yes" or "no." Then write a sentence that provides support for your answer.

> If luck is actually not real, from a scientific perspective, does this mean that the concept has no value or usefulness for guiding how we should act?

_____

_____

_____

_____

③ 06 CD

POINT OF INTEREST

Listen carefully to the audio recording for this section and fill in the blanks in the paragraph below.

Machiavelli studied and wrote extensively about ancient Rome, and so it is no surprise that his 1.) _____ of luck was influenced by the Roman understanding of luck. In ancient Rome, luck was not seen as completely random chance or inexplicably mystical, but rather, it was seen as a 2.) _____ force personified by a goddess named Fortuna. The goddess Fortuna would 3.) _____ bestow good luck or bad luck in a completely capricious way. In other 4.) _____ she rewarded certain behaviors with good luck, and other behaviors with bad luck. A good example of the belief in Fortuna awarding luck based on behavior comes from the classic Roman proverb, 5.) _____ iterated in Virgil's Aeneid as *audentis Fortuna iuvat*—a Latin phrase commonly translated as "fortune favors the bold."

IN THE BEGINNING

What is the link between religion and cosmology?

多くの宗教には、人間や宇宙がどのように生まれたかを説明する「起源説」があるが、それらは一般的に科学的な研究に根ざしたものではない。宇宙がどのようにして生まれたかについての現在の有力な宇宙論は、実はキリスト教の司祭によって定式化されたものである。宇宙論と宗教はどのような関係にあるのだろうか。

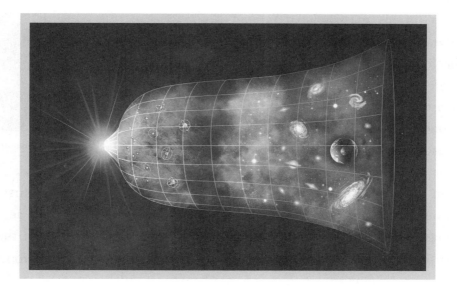

According to the standard version of the Big Bang theory, the universe sprang up from a single point and began to expand, and then galaxies, stars, and planets eventually formed.

GETTING STARTED

Think about the question below and then write a short response. There is no right or wrong answer here, so feel free to write the first thing that comes to mind.

When you take a moment to think about it, what question relating to the mysteries of the universe do you find most intriguing?

_____

_____

READING

07

1 Most religions feature some type of origin story that explains how people and the universe itself came into existence. The *Bible*, for instance, starts off by stating: "In the beginning God created the heaven and the earth." Christian philosophers have long wrestled with this claim that God created the universe. In *The City of*
5 *God*, for example, Augustine of Hippo highlights that God creating the universe means that God's existence predates the existence of the universe, and this leads
him to ultimately conclude that God must have always existed. Eight hundred years later, in his massive text *Summa*
10 *Theologiae*, the medieval philosopher and theologian Thomas Aquinas tried using logic to prove this supposition that God's existence is eternal. Out of his five proofs one is particularly noteworthy
15 here: everything that happens must be caused by something. If we go back far

A burst of sunlight is often seen as a metaphor for creation.

enough in time in the history of the universe, we would have to get to a first cause, which would have not been caused by anything else—and only God, according to Aquinas, could exist without being caused by something. Finally, in the early
20 twentieth century, another Christian thinker, a Belgian priest and astrophysicist named Georges Lemaître, worked on mathematical calculations to understand the state of the universe. The implications of his calculations went far beyond the realm of theological debate, however, for as we will see in this chapter, Lemaître proposed a **ground-breaking**[1] cosmological theory that fundamentally changed our
25 understanding of the universe.

08

2 Lemaître's calculations indicated to him that the universe is expanding, in which case it had to have been smaller in the past. Accordingly, if we were to look back in time far enough, we would eventually find that the universe had to have been all condensed into one spot, which he called a primeval atom. The universe
30 itself, then, had to have started its expansion from this one spot. Lemaître's theory, however, contradicted the prevalent belief in the scientific community at the time that the universe was static. One notable example of a **prominent**[2] scientist who firmly believed in a static universe was none other than Albert Einstein, arguably the twentieth century's most influential theoretical physicist. Even though his own

theory of general relativity indicated that the universe must indeed be expanding, Einstein was so firm in his belief in a static universe that he actually modified his theoretical work so that it would fit with a static model of the universe. When it later became clear that the universe is indeed expanding, as Lemaître calculated, he allegedly called the reason for his decision to modify his theory the "greatest 5 blunder" of his career.

09 🎧CD

3 A series of scientific discoveries helped establish what became known as the Big Bang theory as the leading scientific explanation for how the known universe came to be what it is today. Most notably, two years after Lemaître outlined his theory, American astronomer Edwin Hubble's astronomical observations revealed 10 that other galaxies are in fact moving away from our own galaxy, thereby confirming that the universe is expanding. Then in 1965, two American physicists, Arno Penzias and Robert Wilson, discovered cosmic microwave background radiation (CMBR). Proponents of the Big Bang theory argued that such a massive event should have left some trace of the heat associated with the Big Bang scattered throughout the 15 universe. The CMBR discovered in 1965 turned out to be this trace, essentially confirming the Big Bang theory. In 1966, Lemaître was battling a serious illness, but he survived just long enough to hear the news of the discovery of CMBR, and thus died knowing that his theory of the primeval atom had been essentially confirmed. Recent astronomical observations have even made it possible to calculate the age of 20 the visible universe, which is nearly fourteen billion years old.

10 🎧CD

4 To put it crudely, then, approximately fourteen billion years ago the universe as we know it had yet to form. An unimaginably minuscule "nugget," as physicist Brian Greene puts it, then materialized out of what are still unknown conditions. This nugget essentially inflated to massive proportions almost instantaneously, and 25 after this infinitesimally brief fraction of a second the universe began to cool and expand at a rate comparable to the kind of expansion we see today. Over time, matter aggregated in some regions due to gravitational attraction, which made it possible for galaxies and stars to form. To cap off this story, we could simply summarize that in one part of the universe, some of this matter pulled together to form a galaxy that we 30 call the Milky Way, within which a star that we call the Sun formed, around which a planet that we call Earth formed over four billion years ago.

11 🎧CD

5 As far as the history of the universe is concerned, then, it should come as no surprise that it was a priest-astrophysicist who formulated the basic principles of the Big Bang theory, given that both Christianity and science envision a first mover, 35 albeit of very different sorts. Science and religion therefore offer explanations for how things came to be, but they cannot truly explain why anything exists at all. While some may hail the **magnificent**[3] scientific breakthroughs that explain so much about the history of the universe, we

5 must remember that science cannot explain everything. The Big Bang theory, Greene notes, only tells us what happened a split second after the universe came into existence. This

地動説が発見された話について、章末の Point of Interest を読んでみよう。

cosmological theory is therefore not a theory of cosmic origins, and so it certainly cannot explain why anything exists at all in the first place—and it is this question

10 about why anything exists at all that serves as the focus of the following chapter.

NOTES

wrestle「格闘する」 ***The City of God***「『神の国』」 **Augustine of Hippo**「ヒッポのアウグスチヌス(354–430)ヒッポは現在のアルジェリアのアナバのあたり」 **predate**「先行する、より以前に存在する」 ***Summa Theologiae***「『神学大全』」 **Thomas Aquinas**「トマス・アクィナス (c.1225–1274)」 **supposition**「推測」 **eternal**「永遠の」 **noteworthy**「注目に値する」 **astrophysicist**「天体物理学者」 **Georges Lemaître**「ジョルジュ・ルメートル (1894–1966)」 **cosmological**「宇宙論の」 **condensed**「凝縮した」 **primeval**「根源的」 **contradict**「否定する」 **static**「静止した、変化のない」 **blunder**「大失敗」 **Big Bang theory**「ビッグバン説」 **Edwin Hubble**「エドウィン・ハッブル (1889–1953)」 **Arno Penzias**「アーノ・ペンジアス (1933–)」 **Robert Wilson**「ロバート・ウィルソン (1936–)」 **cosmic microwave background radiation**「宇宙マイクロ波背景放射」 **proponent**「支持者、提唱者」 **crudely**「おおまかに」 **minuscule**「きわめて小さい」 **nugget**「塊」 **inflate**「膨張する」 **instantaneously**「即座に」 **infinitesimally**「ごくわずかに」 **aggregated**「まとめられた」 **cap off**「終える」 **envision**「予見する」 **first mover**「先行者、先発者」 **breakthrough**「大発見」

▌VOCABULARY

For each underlined word below, choose the option that most closely approximates its meaning based on the way that it is used in the reading section.

1. … proposed a <u>ground-breaking</u> cosmological theory …
   a. terrible   **b.** destructive   **c.** revolutionary

2. … example of a <u>prominent</u> scientist who …
   a. famous   **b.** intelligent   **c.** critical

3. … hail the <u>magnificent</u> scientific breakthroughs …
   a. beautiful   **b.** wonderful   **c.** fanciful

COMPREHENSION QUESTIONS

Read each statement below carefully, and then based on the information presented in this chapter, write "T" if it is true or "F" if it is false.

1. _____ In the text *Summa Theologiae*, fifteen of the proofs that Thomas Aquinas formulates are particularly noteworthy.

2. _____ The universe began to expand from one spot, which Georges Lemaître called a primeval atom.

3. _____ Edwin Hubble helped prove what came to be known as the Big Bang theory when he confirmed that the universe is expanding.

4. _____ From the moment the universe sprang into existence it has been expanding at comparable rate to what we see today.

5. _____ Studying the history of the universe reveals that science and religion present the same sort of first mover explanation.

PUTTING IT ALL TOGETHER

For each paragraph in the reading section, compose one complete sentence that summarizes the main theme of that paragraph.

Paragraph 1: _____

_____

Paragraph 2: _____

_____

Paragraph 3: _____

_____

Paragraph 4: _____

_____

Paragraph 5: _____

_____

Write a complete sentence that states whether your answer to the question below is "yes" or "no." Then write a sentence that provides support for your answer.

> Does the Big Bang theory tell us everything about the history of the universe, including its actual origin?

_____

_____

_____

_____

③ 12 CD

POINT OF INTEREST

Listen carefully to the audio recording for this section and fill in the blanks in the paragraph below.

The biblical view of Earth's origins and its place in the universe stood as 1.) _____ in the Western world up until the mid-sixteenth century, when scientific discoveries began to dismantle the Christian understanding of the universe. Nicolaus Copernicus, in a book he posthumously published in 1543, proposed a heliocentric model of the Solar System, which means that it is Earth that orbits the Sun, not the other way around as 2.) _____ generations had assumed. In the early seventeenth century, Johannes Kepler helped confirm heliocentrism, and in the process also 3.) _____ that the planets orbit the Sun elliptically. Kepler's success was in part due to the astronomical observations gathered by a Danish astronomer named Tycho Brahe, who holds the dubious 4.) _____ of having worn a prosthetic metal nose on account of having lost his real nose during a swordfight over a disagreement about a math problem. Around the same time, Italian scientist Galileo Galilei's astronomical observations 5.) _____ the existence of moons orbiting the planet Jupiter, which further supported the heliocentric model's validity by visually confirming that not everything orbits around Earth.

STARING INTO THE ABYSS

Why is there something instead of nothing?

そもそも何かが存在するということは、本当に驚くべきことである。私たちが知っているような広大で物質に満ちた宇宙の代わりに、無限で永続的な無の状態が存在する可能性がある。無の状態は、物質とエネルギーで満たされた宇宙と同じくらい、いや、それ以上に、永遠で無限の空虚の単純さゆえに、あり得ることのように思われる。なぜ何もないのではなく、何かがあるのか。

Death Valley, California, features one of the harshest climates on Earth. Its desolate atmosphere makes it, in some ways, a fitting backdrop for thinking about nothingness.

▌ GETTING STARTED

Think about the question below and then write a short response. There is no right or wrong answer here, so feel free to write the first thing that comes to mind.

How would you describe what is inside an airtight sealed container that appears completely empty?

_____

_____

READING

13

1 The fact that anything exists at all is truly amazing. Instead of the vast and substance-filled realm that is the universe as we know it, there could lie in its stead a state of infinite and perpetual nothingness. This brings us to what many philosophers refer to as the fundamental question: why is there something instead of nothing?

5 Gottfried Wilhelm von Leibniz, a German philosopher and mathematician, may have been the first person to **explicitly**[1] formulate this question in these words, in an essay he wrote in 1714, but the general idea behind this question has surely fascinated countless generations before him, and it is a question that continues to intrigue philosophers and scientists to this day. It seems as though a state of nothingness is

10 just as probable as a universe filled with matter and energy, if not more so due to the sheer simplicity of an eternal and infinite void, so let us take a closer look at this challenging question to see how we can make sense of it.

14

2 One challenge that we experience right off the bat when dealing with a question like this is the inherent difficulty in trying to conceptualize nothingness.

15 Try as we may, we cannot actually visualize, identify, or label nothingness. The very act of defining "nothing" seemingly constitutes it as something. We might therefore define "nothing" as a state where there is no something of any kind whatsoever. To that end, we can envision an imaginary box in which there is

20 no air, no energy, and no subatomic particle of any kind. This would certainly bring us close to the idea of **genuine**[2] nothingness, but this is simply defining "nothing" by what it is not. The problem, then, is that we cannot conceptualize "nothing" without doing so

25 in reference to something. Genuine nothingness would therefore apparently require not only the absence of physical stuff, like particles and energy, but it would also require having nobody around to define it. Further complicating any effort to imagine true nothingness,

30 Albert Einstein's general theory of relativity, which explains how gravitational fields warp space-time, has further altered our understanding of what we think

If we take a moment to ponder the world around us, it can seem truly wondrous that anything at all exists.

of as empty space. This theory has numerous implications, but one implication is especially significant for our purposes here. Whereas we intuitively think that empty space is nothingness, Einstein's work indicates that even empty space is something.

15 🎧 CD

3 Setting aside the difficulties of trying to conceptualize genuine nothingness, the fundamental question raises a metaphorical question that has likely confounded just about everyone at one time or another. Which came first: the chicken or the egg? This question is perplexing for a very obvious reason. If the chicken came first 5 and laid the egg, then where did the chicken come from? If the egg came first and hatched to become the chicken, then where did the egg come from? At first glance, the Big Bang model of the universe seems to indicate that the egg came first, so to speak, in the sense that an infinitesimally small bit of somethingness may very well have spontaneously materialized out of what seems like nothingness, and then this 10 infinitesimally small bit of somethingness went on to grow into the universe that we see today, as the previous chapter addresses.

16 🎧 CD

4 Yet this makes the fact that there is something instead of nothing all the more beguiling. If we postulate that there was true nothingness before the universe as we know it came into existence, it seems inconceivable for something to have been 15 created out of nothing since it would mean that there was no cause for its creation. One way to escape this problem is by **proposing**[3] that the state of nothingness, from which the initial substance spontaneously materialized, was not actually nothingness. Of course this means that if it was not true nothingness that existed prior to the universe spontaneously materializing, then this apparent nothingness was actually something. This something would then have had to have been created by something else, thus simply raising the same question about

> 宇宙が存在する前の世界に関する神話について、章末のPoint of Interestを読んでみよう。

20

where this something else came from—and this line of questioning could go on and on ad infinitum. Alternatively, we could postulate that this something from which 25 the universe emerged has always existed, but this would then simply bring us back to the fundamental question.

17 🎧 CD

5 Clearly, then, neither solution satisfactorily helps us understand why there is something rather than nothing. The explanation that something of some sort has always existed is hard to accept since the idea that something has simply always 30 existed without having been created by something else is counterintuitive. The idea that something came into existence from true nothingness in a creation event at some point long ago also seems like an unacceptable proposition, since this leaves us asking what created the conditions that created the initial substance that grew into the universe? In his book *Beyond Good and Evil*, the nineteenth-century German 35

philosopher Friedrich Nietzsche warns: "when you stare for a long time into an abyss, the abyss stares back into you." Nietzsche's statement is meant as a word of caution that in a way may apply here, insofar as questions such as these can lead to unpleasant findings. In this case, the fundamental question exposes the harsh reality
5 that existence may well be something that is simply inexplicable. Even worse about this question, it is not simply that no one has yet found the answer, but rather, this kind of question is almost certainly just plain unanswerable. The question of why there is something instead of nothing will therefore surely forever remain an unsolved mystery, no matter what scientific advances and technological innovations arise in
10 the future—and in this way it is a question that will likely remain intellectually stimulating for as long as people are around to ponder the nature of existence.

NOTES

perpetual「永遠の」　**Gottfried Wilhelm von Leibniz**「ゴットフリート・ヴィルヘルム・フォン・ライプニッツ (1646 – 1716)」　**fascinate**「魅了する」　**intrigue**「好奇心をそそる」　**right off the bat**「直ちに」 **subatomic**「原子スケール以下の」　**warp**「ゆがめる」　**intuitively**「直感的に」　**metaphorical**「隠喩的、比喩 的」　**confound**「当惑させる」　**perplexing**「困惑させる」　**spontaneously**「自然に」　**materialize**「現れる」 **beguiling**「魅力的な」　**inconceivable**「想像を絶する」　**ad infinitum**「無限に」　**alternatively**「あるいは また」　**counterintuitive**「直観に反した」　***Beyond Good and Evil***「『善悪の彼岸』」　**Friedrich Nietzsche** 「フリードリヒ・ニーチェ (1844 – 1900)」　**plain**「まったく」

◤ VOCABULARY

For each underlined word below, choose the option that most closely approximates its meaning based on the way that it is used in the reading section.

1. … first person to <u>explicitly</u> formulate this …
    a. rudely　　　　　　**b.** directly　　　　　**c.** strangely

2. … close to the idea of <u>genuine</u> nothingness …
    a. actual　　　　　　**b.** mysterious　　　　**c.** complicated

3. … is by <u>proposing</u> that the state of …
    a. dismissing　　　　**b.** inquiring　　　　　**c.** suggesting

COMPREHENSION QUESTIONS

Read each statement below carefully, and then based on the information presented in this chapter, write "T" if it is true or "F" if it is false.

1. _____ Gottfried Leibniz is the first person to think about and wonder about why something exists at all instead of nothing.

2. _____ According to Albert Einstein's theory, even what looks like empty space is actually something.

3. _____ When thinking about the origin of the universe as a chicken-and-egg question, the Big Bang model suggests that the chicken came first.

4. _____ Proving that the nothingness before the Big Bang was actually something would allow us to answer the fundamental question.

5. _____ Nietzsche's quote is meant to remind readers that thinking deeply about some questions can result in unsettling discoveries.

PUTTING IT ALL TOGETHER

For each paragraph in the reading section, compose one complete sentence that summarizes the main theme of that paragraph.

Paragraph 1: _____

_____

Paragraph 2: _____

_____

Paragraph 3: _____

_____

Paragraph 4: _____

_____

Paragraph 5: _____

_____

DEBATING THE ISSUES

Write a complete sentence that states whether your answer to the question below is "yes" or "no." Then write a sentence that provides support for your answer.

> Will the fundamental question likely end up being answered one day when science makes more progress?

_____

_____

_____

_____

③ 18 CD

POINT OF INTEREST

Listen carefully to the audio recording for this section and fill in the blanks in the paragraph below.

Different religious 1.) _____ have long presented a wide array of interesting explanations for the origin of the universe. The ancient Greek poet Hesiod, for example, 2.) _____ that in the beginning was chaos. What exactly he meant by "chaos" in his epic poem *Theogony* is debatable, but it comes down to a fairly simple point of origin: the universe emerged from what we can think of as either a massive formless pool of 3.) _____ or from some infinite void. This represents a simple enough creation myth, one that posits a spontaneous emergence event, followed by a sequence of events that 4.) _____ to humanity's creation. It also suggests that the universe essentially came from nothing, and that godly forces then shaped the world and its contents into what the Greeks 5.) _____ around them—in a very basic way similar to the Big Bang theory discussed in the previous chapter.

CONDEMNED TO BE FREE

Is free will just an illusion?

因果的決定論とは、どんな小さな出来事も、自然の法則によって決定された因果関係の結果であるとするものである。もし、人の心も同じように因果関係によって導かれているとしたら、人間は基本的に物理的な世界の他のものと変わらないということになる。人間には本当に選択の自由があるのだろうか、それとも自由意志は単なる幻想なのか。

French philosopher and author Jean-Paul Sartre is one of the most famous intellectual figures of the twentieth century, and one of his most thought-provoking claims is that human individuals are "condemned to be free.

◀ GETTING STARTED

Think about the question below and then write a short response. There is no right or wrong answer here, so feel free to write the first thing that comes to mind.

If you were lost and encountered two completely identical paths, one leading left and one leading right, how would you choose which path to take?

_____

_____

READING

19

1 In the early nineteenth century, a French mathematician named Pierre-Simon Laplace published an influential text titled *A Philosophical Essay on Probabilities*, in which he has his readers imagine a hypothetical **supreme**[1] being that has the ability to know the location and velocity of every single atom in the universe. Since
5 everything in the universe is bound by the laws of nature, such a being would theoretically be able to calculate everything that will ever happen in the future. "We ought then to regard the present state of the universe," Laplace argues, "as the effect of its anterior state and as the cause of the one which is to follow." In other words, every single thing that happens now is the result of something that happened in the
10 past, and every single thing that happens now will cause something else to happen in the future. This is known as causal determinism, and it underpins our scientific understanding of the physical world. Causal determinism has serious implications for our understanding of human existence, for it raises an important question: are the choices that we make also causally determined? If a person's mind is also guided
15 by the same cause-and-effect sequences that dictate how the physical world operates, it would seem that we are fundamentally no different than anything else in the universe—thus making free will just an illusion. Let us therefore take a closer look at this question to see
20 if free will is indeed just an illusion, or if instead there is something unique about human consciousness that makes free will possible.

Air travel gives people the impression that they are free to choose to go just about anywhere on Earth.

20

2 The free will versus determinism debate is sometimes simply called the problem of free will. At
25 first glance it appears as though free will is possible, and most people would likely reject any notion that their decisions are not actually choices of their own making. Free will seems self-evident, after all, since people who are not **restricted**[2] by physical impediments, whether in the form of
30 physical disabilities or incarceration, for instance, have countless options from which to choose when it comes to making decisions. Furthermore, people make countless decisions every day, from simple decisions like what and when to eat, to important decisions like where to live and what career to pursue.

21

3 For those who adhere to a determinist view, however, free will is not possible for a couple of reasons. First, free will would necessitate that we genuinely have options when we make decisions, and, secondly, free will would necessitate that we have control over the forces that are responsible for the decisions that we make. The second condition in particular raises a serious problem for anyone who wants to defend free will. Countless forces, over which we seemingly have no control, influence 5 how we make decisions. A confluence of circumstantial, societal, physiological, and psychological factors that lie beyond a person's control shapes everything he or she does at any given moment. If decision-making is the result of these forces that lie beyond a person's control, it appears as though we cannot even satisfy the first condition for free will. After all, if these various forces dictate how people make their 10 decisions at any given time, then people cannot choose anything other than whatever it is they end up choosing, and so people never actually have options when they make a decision.

4 When it comes to counterarguments to the determinist perspective, many different perspectives exist, but for the sake of simplicity it is possible to divide them 15 into two broad categories: libertarianism and compatibilism. Libertarians argue that the laws of nature do not necessarily apply to human consciousness, thereby making free will possible. The human mind, libertarians generally argue, is subject to a different kind of causation, one that makes it possible for people to truly choose freely. Compatibilists, on the other hand, accept that 20 determinism does indeed apply to human consciousness, but argue that free will is nevertheless possible. One example of a compatibilist argument entails **distinguishing**[3] between two types of desires. First, there are desires over which we have no control, such as when and what we want to eat. Then there are desires that 25 we form about the desires that we cannot control. For instance, we may not be able to control our desire to eat a lot of unhealthy snacks, but we can perhaps wish that we did not desire to eat junk food. In this way, then, according to the compatibilist perspective, we can freely choose to either act on or refuse to act on the desires that we cannot control. 30

サルトルの自由意志について、章末の Point of Interest を読んでみよう。

5 The free will problem is the subject of intense debate in academia, and understandably so given that philosophers can make a strong case for either perspective. The significance of this debate goes well beyond intellectual curiosity, for adhering to one perspective over the other leads to a dramatically different view of human existence. On the one hand, humans may be seen as extraordinarily complex 35 automatons, insofar as a person's decisions are merely the product of incredibly complex neurochemical reactions and countless cause-and-effect sequences. On the other hand, a person may instead be seen as a being whose consciousness is not subject to the forces that act on the rest of the material world, but rather, is subject to a form of causation that is *sui generis*, which is a Latin phrase that essentially means something like "its own unique type." The view of human existence that results from this debate is quite significant in a practical sense, for it has implications for whether or not people are truly responsible for their own actions, and thus by extension, whether or not it is appropriate to morally judge people for what they do or do not do. Ultimately, which perspective to support, like many other intensely debated issues in life, is something that everyone has to research and figure out on his or her own.

NOTES

Pierre-Simon Laplace「ピエール＝シモン・ラプラス(1749–1827)」 *A Philosophical Essay on Probabilities*「『確率の哲学的試論』」 **hypothetical**「仮想の」 **theoretically**「理論上は」 **anterior**「先行する」 **causal determinism**「因果的決定論」 **underpin**「支える」 **fundamentally**「基本的に」 **impediment**「障害」 **physical disability**「身体障害」 **incarceration**「投獄、拘禁」 **adhere**「固持する」 **necessitate**「余儀なくさせる」 **confluence**「結合、合体」 **counterargument**「反論」 **libertarianism**「リバタリアニズム、自由至上主義、完全自由主義」 **compatibilism**「両立主義、両立論」 **causation**「因果関係」 **entail**「伴う」 **academia**「学問の世界」 **automaton**「ロボット」 **neurochemical**「神経化学の」

◀ VOCABULARY

For each underlined word below, choose the option that most closely approximates its meaning based on the way that it is used in the reading section.

1. … a hypothetical <u>supreme</u> being that has …
   a. prominent   **b.** powerful   **c.** possible

2. … people who are not <u>restricted</u> by physical …
   a. hindered   **b.** motivated   **c.** defeated

3. … entails <u>distinguishing</u> between two types of …
   a. challenging   **b.** differentiating   **c.** visualizing

COMPREHENSION QUESTIONS

Read each statement below carefully, and then based on the information presented in this chapter, write "T" if it is true or "F" if it is false.

1. _____ Pierre-Simon Laplace's view of the universe can be described as what is called causal determinism.

2. _____ The intense philosophical debate surrounding discussions about free will and determinism is sometimes called the free will problem.

3. _____ The freedom to make a choice may actually be impossible since forces beyond a person's control influence how he or she chooses.

4. _____ Libertarians argue that we cannot control our desires, but we can control how we react to those desires.

5. _____ The debate surrounding free will is important for understanding human existence, but it has no broader implications.

PUTTING IT ALL TOGETHER

For each paragraph in the reading section, compose one complete sentence that summarizes the main theme of that paragraph.

Paragraph 1: _____

_____

Paragraph 2: _____

_____

Paragraph 3: _____

_____

Paragraph 4: _____

_____

Paragraph 5: _____

_____

Write a complete sentence that states whether your answer to the question below is "yes" or "no." Then write a sentence that provides support for your answer.

> Given that the deterministic perspective is rooted in a scientific understanding of the world, is it more convincing than the other perspectives?

_____

_____

_____

_____

③ 24 CD

POINT OF INTEREST

Listen carefully to the audio recording for this section and fill in the blanks in the paragraph below.

Although not deeply engaged in the technical details and the minutiae of the various arguments in the free will 1.) _____, the French philosopher Jean-Paul Sartre is perhaps the most famous defender of the free will perspective. He bluntly 2.) _____, in his magnum opus *Being and Nothingness*, that human individuals are "condemned to be free," and by "free" he means free to make choices, and by "condemned" he means that "we are not free to cease to be free." This view is part of his 3.) _____ existentialist treatise, wherein he argues that "existence precedes essence." What this 4.) _____ means is that a person's essence—one's identity and value system—is not the product of an established human identity that is set before a person is even born, but is instead forged by the choices he or she makes over the course of a lifetime. By way of 5.) _____, a wild animal has a set behavioral pattern that is largely predetermined based on the genetic traits of its species, and so what this animal will be like is already mostly set before it is even born.

END OF THE ROAD

How is it all going to end?

宇宙物理学者は、太陽が数十億年後に燃料を使い果たし始め、その時点でいわゆる赤色巨星に膨張し、その外層は最終的に地球の表面を完全に焦がすか、あるいは地球を完全に飲み込んでしまうと考えている。SF では、恒星間移動が日常的で簡単に行われている未来がよく描かれる。太陽が消滅する前に人類は太陽系を脱出できるのか。脱出できたとして、人類は未来に無限に生存できるのか。

All good things must come to an end. This expression usually refers to specific events in life, but it perhaps even applies to the universe itself.

▶ GETTING STARTED

Think about the question below and then write a short response. There is no right or wrong answer here, so feel free to write the first thing that comes to mind.

How do you think you will feel about your time as a university student after you graduate and move on to the next stage of your life?

_____

_____

READING

25

1 All good things, the old adage goes, must come to an end. This old adage even appears set to apply to the Sun, which astrophysicists believe will begin to run out of fuel in a few billion years. It will then begin to **swell**[1] into what is called a red giant, at which point its outer layers will eventually completely scorch Earth's surface
5 or perhaps even engulf the planet entirely. The Sun will then cool off and essentially die, rendering the Solar System uninhabitable. This raises an obvious question: will humanity manage to establish a presence far beyond the Solar System by the time the Sun begins to die, and if so, could humanity go on forever by continually finding new habitable worlds? As this chapter will demonstrate, even if humanity
10 could continually expand its presence to new planets, scientific theories about the ultimate fate of the universe indicate that, one way or another, human existence will eventually come to an end.

26

2 Before wondering about the distant future after the Sun dies billions of years from now, it is worth remembering that humanity faces far more imminent
15 threats to its existence. Several potential manmade disasters could very well imperil life on Earth, ranging from, for instance, runaway anthropogenic climate change to thermonuclear world war. Even if we give humanity the benefit of the doubt
20 that leaders from around the world will collaborate to ensure that such manmade catastrophes do not befall our planet, one natural threat in particular could threaten the very existence of life on Earth, and
25 there is currently no way to defend against it: a large asteroid. Scientists estimate that

The threat of a large asteroid colliding with Earth represents one of the few hazards that could instantaneously end human existence.

an asteroid impact large enough to threaten life on Earth likely occurs once every few million years. It may seem trivial given the rarity of such an event, but the large asteroid that slammed into Earth approximately sixty-six million years ago should
30 serve as a reminder of this threat's severity. This asteroid created the Chicxulub crater that lies beneath the Yucatán Peninsula in Mexico, and the impact was so catastrophic that it triggered a mass extinction event, which notably included most dinosaur species.

27

3 Even if humanity survives long enough to develop the technology needed to leave the Solar System, Albert Einstein's theory of special relativity indicates that a "cosmic speed limit" will restrict how far humans can travel. According to special relativity, as an object approaches the speed of light, its mass increases, and if an object were to reach light speed its mass would become infinite. This means that infinite energy would be required in order to power whatever propulsion system would be used to **sustain**[2] this velocity. Even if humans could achieve anything close to light speed, which is approximately 1.08 billion kilometers per hour, the vastness of space would make it incredibly difficult for humanity to settle extraterrestrial worlds. For instance, even at light speed it would take four years to reach the Sun's nearest stellar neighbor, Proxima Centauri, and it is currently unclear if any of its three exoplanets that astronomers have detected so far are even habitable. Space travel within the bounds of this scientific principle is therefore incredibly limited, and so unless new scientific discoveries reveal that it is somehow possible to travel faster than light, continually reaching and populating other habitable planets could be virtually impossible.

4 There is of course no telling how far human beings might advance scientifically and technologically in the future, which could thus turn our understanding of what is possible completely on its head. Nevertheless, even if humanity somehow develops the ability to exceed the speed of light, thereby achieving interstellar travel similar to the kind portrayed in the *Star Trek* television series and films, human existence may nevertheless still be doomed. The reason for this is that the universe is expanding, and the rate of expansion is increasing. Consequently, many theoretical physicists hypothesize that the universe itself is destined to essentially end in the inconceivably distant future. According to one theory, dubbed the "Big Rip," the accelerating expansion of the universe will eventually cause everything in the universe to effectively rip apart. This process will mark the end of existence, for it will not only be stars and other large-scale stellar objects that will rip apart, but even matter itself at the subatomic level. Another hypothesis, dubbed the "Big Freeze," indicates that all star formation will eventually cease as the supply of gas in the universe runs out, resulting in the heat death of the universe, and, in practical terms, the end of existence.

5 Ultimately, while different theoretical models propose different processes for how the universe will end, they all propose a similar outcome: vast emptiness where for all intents and purposes everything has ceased to exist. Pondering the ultimate fate of the universe is intriguing, insofar as such a fascinating topic beckons our intellectual curiosity, but in some ways it seems as though such discussions hold no practical relevance today. Surviving long enough to become a centenarian, though increasingly common, is still quite rare for human beings, and living a decade or two past that is exceedingly rare. In fact, the oldest recorded human lifespan is that of Jeanne Calment, a French woman who reached 122 years old. From this perspective, what happens to humanity, or even the universe itself, in the unimaginably distant

5　future matters not to anyone alive today. Even though this line of thought deals with events that will not occur until long after we are gone, and even though there is no **guarantee**[3] that events will play out as these theories project, the idea that the universe is seemingly destined for oblivion is a key

10　factor in perhaps one of the most important questions of all: what is the meaning of life? It is this question to which we turn in the next, and final, chapter of this book.

> 寿命を延ばすための遺伝子研究について、章末の Point of Interest を読んでみよう。

NOTES

red giant「赤色巨星」　　**scorch**「焦がす」　　**engulf**「飲み込む」　　**imminent**「差し迫った」　　**imperil**「危険にさらす」　　**runaway**「制御できない」　　**anthropogenic**「人間 (の活動) に起因する」　　**thermonuclear**「水素爆弾を利用する」　　**collaborate**「協力する」　　**befall**「降りかかる」　　**asteroid**「小惑星」　　**trivial**「些細な」　　**slam**「激突する」　　**severity**「激しさ」　　**Chicxulub crater**「チクシュルーブ・クレーター」　　**extinction**「絶滅」　　**dinosaur**「恐竜」　　**propulsion**「推進」　　**extraterrestrial**「地球大気圏外の」　　**stellar**「星の」　　**Proxima Centauri**「プロキシマ・ケンタウリ」　　**exoplanet**「太陽系外惑星」　　**turn ~ on its head**「~を覆す」　　**hypothesize**「仮説を立てる」　　**inconceivably**「考えられないほど」　　**dub**「名前を付ける」　　**Big Rip**「ビッグリップ」　　**rip**「裂ける」　　**Big Freeze**「ビッグフリーズ」　　**heat death**「熱 (力学) 的死 (宇宙の最後の状態)」　　**ponder**「熟考する」　　**intriguing**「興味をそそる」　　**centenarian**「百歳 (以上) の人」　　**oblivion**「忘却」

◤ VOCABULARY

For each underlined word below, choose the option that most closely approximates its meaning based on the way that it is used in the reading section.

1. … begin to <u>swell</u> into what is called …
   a. enlarge　　　　　**b.** accelerate　　　　　**c.** diverge

2. … would be used to <u>sustain</u> this …
   a. increase　　　　　**b.** maintain　　　　　**c.** function

3. … there is no <u>guarantee</u> that …
   a. promise　　　　　**b.** agreement　　　　　**c.** certainty

COMPREHENSION QUESTIONS

Read each statement below carefully, and then based on the information presented in this chapter, write "T" if it is true or "F" if it is false.

1. _____ Astrophysicists believe the Sun will begin to swell into what is called a red giant in a few million years.

2. _____ An asteroid impact large enough to threaten life on Earth, according to scientists, likely occurs once every few million years.

3. _____ The reason why interstellar travel would be difficult is that we will likely be unable to travel at the speed of light.

4. _____ Even if humans master interstellar travel and settle planets throughout the universe, humanity likely will eventually cease to exist.

5. _____ The ultimate fate of humanity only seems relevant if we can reach the oldest recorded human lifespan of 122 years old.

PUTTING IT ALL TOGETHER

For each paragraph in the reading section, compose one complete sentence that summarizes the main theme of that paragraph.

Paragraph 1: _____

_____

Paragraph 2: _____

_____

Paragraph 3: _____

_____

Paragraph 4: _____

_____

Paragraph 5: _____

_____

Write a complete sentence that states whether your answer to the question below is "yes" or "no." Then write a sentence that provides support for your answer.

Does it seem likely that humans will still be around in the incredibly distant future when the universe is projected to end?

_____

_____

_____

_____

③ 30 CD

POINT OF INTEREST

Listen carefully to the audio recording for this section and fill in the blanks in the paragraph below.

In a paper titled "Reprogramming to 1.) _____ youthful epigenetic information and restore vision," published in 2020 in the journal *Nature*, a team of geneticists discuss the results of their experiment on mice that successfully reverted old cells to earlier versions of themselves. The experiment focused on the eyesight of mice, whereby an old mouse with poor eyesight had its vision restored to the level that it had when it was in its 2.) _____. Some researchers believe that the cellular process applied to the experimental mouse's eyesight could apply to its 3.) _____ body, which could essentially rejuvenate an old mouse to a youthful state. What is especially 4.) _____ is that some researchers believe that this process could perhaps end up eventually applying to the human body, and so these findings offer some hope that the aging process can one day be slowed down, and perhaps even be reversed. This kind of research could thus end up being the first step to one day eventually 5.) _____ what has long been the most desired, yet the most elusive, thing ever pursued—eternal life.

IN THE GRAND SCHEME OF THINGS

What is the meaning of life?

はるか遠い未来のことではあるが、宇宙そのものが消滅する可能性がある。結局は最後にすべて失われるのであれば、そもそも物事に一体何の意味があるのかという疑問が湧いてくる。自分の存在意義を大局的に捉えることはもちろん難しいが、人生において充実感を得るためには重要な問題である。人生の意味をどのように見出したらいいのだろうか。

Visiting an inspiring place like the Grand Canyon, located in the state of Arizona, can be quite helpful for thinking about the meaning of life.

GETTING STARTED

Think about the question below and then write a short response. There is no right or wrong answer here, so feel free to write the first thing that comes to mind.

What is the most important thing to have, as in, for example, a good career, or good friends, in order for someone to find life satisfying?

_____

_____

◤ READING

1 The term "meaning" in the context of the "meaning of life" refers to a person's sense of purpose and the desire for significance in the grand scheme of things. Assessing one's own significance in the grand scheme of things is obviously challenging, given that, as the previous chapter explains, the universe itself may
5 ultimately cease to exist in the incredibly distant future. This brings up an obvious question: what is the point of anything if it is likely all the same in the end? This chapter presents a novel way of thinking about the meaning of life by suggesting that people can find meaning in life on three levels, and
10 as a way to help guide our quest to make sense of this question about the meaning of life, we will use Homer's epic poem the *Odyssey* as a narrative aid to help clarify each level. Determining what constitutes a meaningful life, as this chapter ultimately demonstrates, is in some
15 ways not as complicated as it seems, while in other ways it is perhaps even more challenging than one might anticipate.

2 The *Odyssey* recounts the long and perilous trek that Odysseus, King of Ithaca, makes to get back
20 home to his wife and son in Greece after ten years of fighting abroad. On the way home, Odysseus gets

This gargoyle sculpture that sits atop the Notre Dame Cathedral in Paris has a facial expression that connotes being dejected, but pensive as well.

the opportunity of a lifetime when he meets the goddess Calypso, who offers to make him immortal as long as he agrees to stay with her **eternally**[1] on her island. The opportunity to live forever would surely make it easy for Odysseus to find a
25 sense of meaning from countless momentary pleasures. He could, for instance, enjoy simply being alive, and forever enjoy the beauty of the island's shores. This brings us to the first level of meaning in life: satisfaction from simply existing and living in the moment. Enjoying beautiful things in life, being outdoors in nature, spending time with friends and family, and even enduring certain emotionally challenging
30 experiences, for example, all make life meaningful in the moment when such events are being experienced.

3 It seems, however, that there is more to life than merely enjoying being alive in the moment. Returning to the example of the *Odyssey*, immortality would indeed free Odysseus from eventually dying, but staying alone with Calypso would make his life inconsequential. Back in Ithaca, on the other hand, he would have objectives to achieve: as king, he could work on making Ithaca prosperous; as a father, he could work on seeing his son **mature**[2] properly; and as a military commander, he could strive to defeat his enemies. After living with Calypso on the island for seven years, Odysseus therefore decides to leave, which brings us to the second level of meaning in life: setting specific objectives that create the parameters through which people can find meaning. Setting goals makes it possible for a person's actions to have actual significance relative to the parameters he or she defines. If someone is playing a game of chess, for example, each and every move he or she makes is significant in the context of a defined objective, namely, winning the game. Similarly, if someone sets a goal of sailing around the world, then each and every mile covered during the journey matters insofar as it contributes to the journey's success.

34 CD

4 The kind of meaning found while striving to accomplish certain goals, though, may still not be sufficiently fulfilling for human existence. Returning to the *Odyssey*, the visit that Odysseus and his men make to an island inhabited by a vicious immortal giant, named Polyphemus, reveals that Odysseus wants to be eternally remembered. After Polyphemus traps Odysseus and his men in a cave, the crafty Ithacan king blinds the vicious giant, thereby making an escape possible. Once safely back on his boat, he proudly shouts to Polyphemus back on shore that "Odysseus" is the name of the man who engineered this clever escape. In so doing, Odysseus seemingly achieves yet another level

生きることの意義の第三の段階について、章末のPoint of Interest を読んでみよう。

of meaning in life, for his name will now live on eternally in the immortal giant's memory. This brings us to the third level of meaning: knowing that one's actions in life somehow leave a mark, even long after having left this world. High-profile public figures may seek to secure a place in history that will allow them to be remembered indefinitely, while others who may not have widespread **recognition**[3] may seek to start a family that will continue long after they are gone. Knowing that something will live on after them can give people a sense of meaning in life, for the belief that one's existence has made a difference in the world and that some part of oneself continues in the memory of others offers a sense of significance.

35 CD

5 Ultimately, even those who have found a significant place in history may eventually fade into obscurity. Humanity has thus far produced relatively few noteworthy people over the course of just a few thousand years of recorded history. Hundreds of thousands of years from now, if humanity lasts that long, people will likely not remember anyone that we today consider significant. Even if those who we now consider noteworthy historical figures are somehow remembered in the incredibly distant future, the universe itself will likely eventually cease to exist, for all intents and purposes, as discussed in the previous chapter, and so it appears that there will eventually come a time when there is no one left to remember even the most famous people in history. It therefore seems as though finding meaning on the first two levels discussed in this chapter is far more important than trying to be remembered in the distant future. In the end, then, what exactly is the meaning of life? There is no prescribed path or course of action, but rather, it is up to each person to figure out on his or her own what can make life meaningful on each level covered in this chapter. Regardless of how people ultimately go about figuring this out, it is clear that in light of some of the significant changes to our way of life that have arisen in recent years, it is more important than ever to ponder such an important question—especially for those who are determined to start rethinking the world.

NOTES

Homer「ホメロス、ホーマー（古代ギリシャの詩人、生没年未詳）」　epic「叙事詩」　*Odyssey*「『オデュッセイア』」　perilous「非常に危険な」　trek「苦難の旅」　Odysseus「オデュッセウス」　Ithaca「イタケー（島）」　Calypso「カリプソ」　immortal「不死の」　countless「数えきれない」　momentary「束の間の」　eventually「いつかは」　inconsequential「つまらない」　prosperous「繁栄する」　parameter「要素」　fulfilling「やりがいのある」　vicious「残忍な」　Polyphemus「ポリュフェモス」　engineer「たくらむ」　fade into obscurity「次第に忘れ去られる」

◤ VOCABULARY

For each underlined word below, choose the option that most closely approximates its meaning based on the way that it is used in the reading section.

1. … he agrees to stay with her <u>eternally</u> on …
   a. vastly　　　　**b.** forever　　　　**c.** casually

2. … seeing his son <u>mature</u> properly …
   a. develop　　　　**b.** move　　　　**c.** formulate

3. … widespread <u>recognition</u> may seek to …
   a. respect　　　　**b.** wealth　　　　**c.** fame

◄ COMPREHENSION QUESTIONS

Read each statement below carefully, and then based on the information presented in this chapter, write "T" if it is true or "F" if it is false.

1. _____ When it comes to the expression "meaning of life," the term "meaning" refers to people's longing for significance.

2. _____ Calypso's offer to Odysseus shows that the first level of meaning is attainable only for those who can achieve immortality.

3. _____ Odysseus rejects Calypso's offer, but only after living with her on the island for seven years.

4. _____ Blinding the vicious giant allowed Odysseus to return to his boat safely and sail away from the island quietly and unnoticed.

5. _____ Trying to be remembered in the distant future is seemingly less important than enjoying life in the moment and setting goals.

◄ PUTTING IT ALL TOGETHER

For each paragraph in the reading section, compose one complete sentence that summarizes the main theme of that paragraph.

Paragraph 1: _____

_____

Paragraph 2: _____

_____

Paragraph 3: _____

_____

Paragraph 4: _____

_____

Paragraph 5: _____

_____

Write a complete sentence that states whether your answer to the question below is "yes" or "no." Then write a sentence that provides support for your answer.

> Does the author suggest that all three levels are equally important to the pursuit of meaning in one's life?

_____

_____

_____

_____

③ 36 CD

◄ **POINT OF INTEREST**

Listen carefully to the audio recording for this section and fill in the blanks in the paragraph below.

Many of history's most notable figures may well have felt a sense of meaning in life from knowing that their 1.) _____ would be remembered. 2.) _____ the Dutch painter Vincent van Gogh, however, who is now one of the most revered painters in art history. Despite his eminent place in history, van Gogh likely could not 3.) _____ the meaning that his life would end up having in a historical sense, for he experienced intense sorrow throughout much of his life and his artistic genius went virtually unnoticed during his own lifetime. On the other hand, countless rulers throughout history enjoyed fame and power while alive and thus surely believed that their legacy would be 4.) _____, yet were completely forgotten after they passed away. Strangely enough, then, it appears that true historical significance offers no sense of meaning if someone is unaware that he or she shall hold a 5.) _____ place in history, while conversely, people falsely believing themselves destined for historical significance can offer them a sense of meaning.

Selected Bibliography

The following sources include classic works and contemporary scholarship. These sources were helpful while writing this book, and may therefore also prove beneficial to students who are interested in learning more about any particular topic covered in the preceding chapters.

Aquinas, Thomas. "Summa contra Gentiles." In *Thomas Aquinas: Selected Writings*, translated by Ralph McInerny. London: Penguin Books, 1968 (orig. pub. 1259).

Aristotle. *The Athenian Constitution*. Translated by P. J. Rhodes. London: Penguin Books, 1984 (orig. pub. c. 332-322 BCE).

Aristotle. *The Art of Rhetoric*. Translated by H.C. Lawson-Tancred. London: Penguin Books, 2004 (orig. c. 367-322 BCE).

Augustine of Hippo. *City of God: Books 8-11*. Translated by David S. Wiesen. Cambridge, MA: Harvard University Press, 1968 (orig. pub. 426 CE).

de Soete, François. "The Advantages of Parliament beyond the *Perils of Presidentialism:* Parliament's Prospects for Indirect Deliberative Democracy." *Memoirs of the Institute of Social Sciences and Humanities, Ritsumeikan University* 96 (2011): 195-223.

de Soete, François. "The Trump Presidency, the Coronavirus, and the New America: Can the U.S. Military Still Preserve the Status Quo in East Asia?" *Journal of International Studies* 10 (2021): 37-52.

de Soete, François. "From a Kingdom of Gold to One of Iron and Rust: Political Violence and the Fall of the Roman Empire." *Kwansei Gakuin University Humanities Review* 26 (2021): 87-106.

de Soete, François. "Plato's Search for Justice: Connecting the Soul, the Forms, and Goodness in the Republic." *Kwansei Gakuin University Social Sciences Review* 26 (2021): 1-18.

de Soete, François. "Trump, Biden, and U.S. Foreign Policy: Analyzing the Role of the Modern Presidency on America's Standing in the World." *Journal of International Studies* 11 (2022): 1-11.

Descartes, René. *Discourse on Method and Related Writings*. Translated by Desmond Clarke. London: Penguin Books, 1999 (orig. pub. 1637).

Descartes, René. *Meditations and Other Metaphysical Writings*. Translated by Desmond Clarke. London: Penguin Books, 1998 (orig. pub. 1641-1649).

Dugatkin, Lee Alan and Trut, Lyudmila. *How to Tame a Fox (and Build a Dog): Visionary Scientists and a Siberian Tale of Jump-Started Evolution*. Chicago: The University of Chicago Press, 2017.

Einstein, Albert. *Relativity: The Special and the General Theory (15th Edition)*. New York: Three Rivers Press, 1961.

Frankfurt, Harry G. "Freedom of the Will and the Concept of a Person." In *Free Will, Second Edition,* edited by Gary Watson, 337-351. Oxford: Oxford University Press, 2003.

Greene, Brian. *The Fabric of the Cosmos: Space, Time, and the Texture of Reality*. New York: Vintage Books, Inc., 2004.

Greene, Brian. *The Hidden Reality: Parallel Universes and the Deep Laws of the Cosmos*. New York: Vintage Books, Inc., 2011.

Hawking, Stephen, and Mlodinow, Leonard. *The Grand Design*. New York: Bantam Books, 2010.

Hesiod. "Theogony." In *Hesiod and Theognis*, translated by Dorothea Wender. London: Penguin Books, 1973 (orig. c. 700 BCE).

Homer. *The Odyssey*. Translated by Robert Fagles. New York: Penguin Books, 1996 (orig. c. 700 BCE)

Horace. "Epistles." In *Satires, Epistles, and Ars of Poetica,* translated by H. Rushton Fairclough. Cambridge, MA: Harvard University Press, 1926 (orig. pub. c. 20 BCE).

Kant, Immanuel. *Critique of Pure Reason*. Translated by Marcus Weigelt. London: Penguin Books Ltd, 2007 (orig. pub. 1781).

Laplace, Pierre Simon Marquis de. *A Philosophical Essay on Probabilities*. Translated by Frederick Wilson Truscott and Frederick Lincoln Emory. New York: John Wiley & Sons, 1902 (orig. pub. 1814).

Leibniz, Gottfried Wilhelm. "Principles of Nature and Grace Based on Reason." In *G. W. Leibniz: Philosophical Essays,* translated by Roger Ariew and Daniel Garber. Indianapolis, IN: Hackett Publishing Company, Inc., 1989.

Lewis, David. "Are We Free to Break the Laws." In *Free Will, Second Edition,* edited by Gary Watson, 337-351. Oxford: Oxford University Press, 2003.

Lorenz, Edward N. *The Essence of Chaos (Jessie and John Danz Lecture)*. Seattle: The University of Washington Press, 1993.

Machiavelli, Niccolò. *The Prince*. Translated by Peter Bondanella. Oxford: Oxford University Press, 2005 (orig. pub. 1532).

Marx, Karl. "The Eighteenth Brumaire of Louis Bonaparte." In *The Portable Karl Marx,* edited by Eugene Kamenka, 287-324. New York: Penguin Books, 1983 (orig. pub. 1852).

Mill, John Stuart. "On Liberty." In *On Liberty and the Subjection of Women,* edited by Alan Ryan, 1-130. New York: Penguin Books, 2006 (orig. pub. 1859).

Nagel, Thomas. "Freedom." In *Free Will, Second Edition,* edited by Gary Watson, 337-351. Oxford: Oxford University Press, 2003.

Nietzsche, Friedrich. *Beyond Good and Evil: Prelude to a Philosophy of the Future*. Translated by Judith Norman. Cambridge: Cambridge University Press, 2002 (orig. pub. 1886).

Ovid. *Metamorphoses: Books 1-8*. Translated by Frank Justus Miller. Cambridge, MA: Harvard University Press, 1916 (orig. pub. 7 CE).

Plato. "Apology." In *The Last Days of Socrates,* translated by Christopher Rowe. New York: Penguin Books, 2010 (orig. pub. c. 390 BCE).

Plato. "Crito." In *Euthyphro, Apology, Crito, Phaedo,* translated by Chris Emlyn-Jones and William Preddy. Cambridge, MA: Harvard University Press, 2017 (orig. pub. c. 390 BCE).

Plato. *Republic: Books 1-5*. Translated by Chris Emlyn-Jones and William Preddy. Cambridge, MA: Harvard University Press, 2013 (orig. pub. c. 370 BCE).

Plato. *Republic: Books 6-10.* Translated by Chris Emlyn-Jones and William Preddy. Cambridge, MA: Harvard University Press, 2013 (orig. pub. c. 370 BCE).

Sartre, Jean-Paul. "Bad Faith." In *Jean-Paul Sartre: Basic Writings,* edited by Stephen Priest, 204-220. New York: Routledge, 2001.

Sartre, Jean-Paul. "Freedom." In *Jean-Paul Sartre: Basic Writings,* edited by Stephen Priest, 177-190. New York: Routledge, 2001.

Sartre, Jean-Paul. *Being and Nothingness: An Essay in Phenomenological Ontology.* Translated by Sarah Richmond. New York: Routledge, 2018 (orig. pub. 1943).

Stannard, Russell. *The End of Discovery: Are We Approaching the Boundaries of the Knowable?* Oxford: Oxford University Press, 2010.

Thucydides. *The Peloponnesian War.* Translated by Martin Hammond. Oxford: Oxford University Press, 2009 (orig. pub. c. 400 BCE).

Tocqueville, Alexis de. "Democracy in America." In *Democracy in America and Two Essays on America,* translated by Gerald E. Bevan. New York: Penguin Books, 2003 (orig. pub. 1835 and 1840).

Virgil. *Aeneid, Books 7-12; Appendix Vergiliana.* Translated by H. R. Fairclough and revised by G. P. Goold. Cambridge, MA: Harvard University Press, 2000 (orig. pub. c. 19 BCE).

Voltaire. *Treatise on Toleration.* Translated by Desmond M. Clarke. New York: Penguin Books, 2016 (orig. pub. 1763).

Voltaire. *Philosophical Dictionary.* Translated by Theodore Besterman. New York: Penguin Books, 2004 (orig. pub. 1764).

Acknowledgements

Katsunosuke Namita, professor emeritus from Hokkaido University, provided the annotations for this textbook, along with the translation for the accompanying teacher's manual. Thank you, Professor Namita, for the immense time and effort that you have devoted, over the span of a full decade now, to the five textbooks on which we have collaborated. Working with you on this fifth book was once again a truly rewarding experience—and it is my sincere hope that we will have an opportunity to collaborate on a future project again soon.

My sincere gratitude also goes out to Seibido, and Mr. Takashi Kudo and Ms. Hiromi Oota in particular for their wonderful editorial support. Thank you both for your time and effort on getting *Rethinking the World* ready for publication.

François de Soete

著者紹介

Dr. François de Soete（政治学博士）

アリゾナ州立大学にて歴史学および政治学の2つの学士号を最優秀で修めたのち、ブリティッシュ・コロンビア大学大学院にて政治学の修士号と博士号を取得。日本および北米の大学で政治哲学や国際関係論の授業を担当し、学術論文の執筆や国際学会における発表を行ってきた。本書は、『民主主義の歩みと現代国家』（2012年）、『現代世界を理解するための視点』（2014年）、『グローバル社会を読み解く新たな視点』（2017年）、『グローバル時代を生き抜く変革への視点』（2020年）に続く成美堂からの5冊目の教科書。

About the Author

Dr. François de Soete graduated summa cum laude from Arizona State University, where he received his B.A. in history and his B.A. in political science. He then pursued his graduate studies at the University of British Columbia, where he earned his M.A. and then his Ph.D. in political science. He has taught courses in political philosophy and international relations in Japan and North America, and has published research articles and presented papers at academic conferences on these topics. This is now his fifth book with Seibido, the prior four being: *Democracy Around the World: Ancient Origins and Contemporary Practices* (2012), *Making Sense of the World: Wisdom Through Knowledge* (2014), *Thinking About Our Place in the World: New Questions, New Answers* (2017), and *Getting Ready to Change the World: New Challenges, New Opportunities* (2020).

TEXT PRODUCTION STAFF

edited by	編集
Takashi Kudo	工藤 隆志
Hiromi Oota	太田 裕美

English-language editing by	英文校閲
Bill Benfield	ビル・ベンフィールド

cover design by	表紙デザイン
Nobuyoshi Fujino	藤野 伸芳

text design by	本文デザイン
Nobuyoshi Fujino	藤野 伸芳

DTP by	DTP
Ruben Frosali	ルーベン・フロサリ

CD PRODUCTION STAFF

recorded by	吹き込み者
Howard Colefield (AmE)	ハワード・コルフィールド（アメリカ英語）
Jennifer Okano (AmE)	ジェニファー・オカノ（アメリカ英語）

Rethinking the World
—Dare to Know—
激動の現代社会を読み解く視点

2023年1月20日　初版発行
2023年2月15日　第2刷発行

著　者　François de Soete
編註者　浪田 克之介
発行者　佐野 英一郎
発行所　株式会社 成美堂
　　　　〒101-0052　東京都千代田区神田小川町3-22
　　　　TEL 03-3291-2261　　　FAX 03-3293-5490
　　　　https://www.seibido.co.jp

印刷・製本　萩原印刷株式会社

ISBN 978-4-7919-7272-2　　　　　　　　　　　　Printed in Japan